W9-CSF-522

Beyond the Tears:

A Story of God's Faithfulness

Clene Nyiramahoro

Beyond the Tears: A Story of God's Faithfulness

Copyright © 2010 Clene Nyiramahoro

Published by:

Integrity Publishers Inc.
P.O. Box 789,
Wake Forest, NC 27588
U.S.A.
info@integritypublishers.org

Printed By:

Tafsiri Printing Press
E: tafsiripress@btlkenya.org

ISBN 13: 978-0-9821175-8-3

ISBN 10: 0-9821175-8-2

Cover Design – Ascent Ltd.

All rights reserved. No part of this book may be reproduced in any form, except for the inclusion of brief quotations in a review, without permission in writing from the author.

Printed in the United States of America. Printed in the United States of America.

All Scripture references are from the The HOLY BIBLE, NEW IN-TERNATIONAL VERSION unless otherwise noted. Copyright ©1973, 1978, 1984 International Bible Society. Used by permission of Zondervan Bible Publishers.

The proceeds of the purchase of this book will be used to further my research on culture and conflict in Africa.

Dedication

To God, in whom I base my pride,

To my husband, who has generously shared his life with me,

To my parents, whose struggles and sacrifices for my sake,

I cherish,

To my children, the living testimonies of our Maker

and Sustainer,

To all the women in Africa who may identify with my story,

I dedicate this book.

Acknowledgements

This book has been a result of much encouragement and support from a number of people who are very dear to me. I may not be able to mention everyone by name but I am so thankful for all of you whose contributions helped make me who I am today.

First, I would like to thank Professor Regina Blass, who after listening to my story encouraged me not only to write this book but also to believe in and discover my potential. Because of your efforts I am where I am today.

Second, my gratitude goes to the entire NEGST community, especially my lecturers for the teaching, mentoring, nourishing and counselling without which I would not been transformed into the usable instrument for God's Kingdom that I believe I am today. Mrs. Cole, thank you so much for making me understand that English was not supposed to be a barrier to my learning, may you receive your deserved appreciation.

Third, my regards go to all my colleagues in PAC University for allowing me to be part of your team. Special thanks go to the Translation Department team led by Elizabeth Olsen, all the other teaching staff, namely David and Estelle Abernathy, Bill and Lori Gardner and Helen Wilson. I miss you dearly. To the women's Bible study group at PAC University for treating me as a sister and a daughter: Joan for being a grandma to my children, Eva for your thoughtfulness, Kim for reading and editing my first draft, Christine and Shelly for your encouragement - you are all highly appreciated. To Catherine Muriuki the PAC University librarian, for your inspiring and encouraging messages, many of which I have used in my last chapter on the lessons learned, may the Lord greatly touch your heart. And to all my friends, receive my expressions of heartfelt gratitude.

Fourth, Mr. Barine for giving me your time to discuss this work and for the guidance you have freely and willingly given me, I have no words to thank you. May the Lord richly bless you.

Last but not least, Ms Mboya, the Director of Ruaraka Academy, and the entire Ruaraka Academy family for giving my children a comfortable learning environment and for treating them as your own. You will be forever remembered for your kindness and your ministry to children.

Table of Contents

Foreword

When I began to read Clene Nyiramahoro's book I imagined it was going to be yet another chronicle of massacres and sadness in Rwanda, albeit from a woman's perspective. To my immense pleasure, while this engaging true story does have its beginning in Rwanda before and during its worst moments, it does not stop there. Rather than focusing our attention on the worst behavior that humans are capable of, Clene's story lifts the reader through a moving account of God's love and provision and faithfulness. Her story clearly demonstrates that life can be renewed and refreshed even after difficult circumstances or tragedies strike.

Although my situation and environment are very different from the ones the author experienced, I easily related to many of the emotions and situations she encountered - a sense of satisfaction at doing well in one's studies, the desire to make a name for oneself professionally, the heady fun of being courted by a handsome young man, the awesome challenge of motherhood as she learned needed skills along the way. I was thoroughly intrigued with the ways God provided for these desires during the course of her story – the desires of our youth may come to fruition in ways we never expected and through paths that only God could have imagined!

Clene also transports her readers to situations that would rattle and challenge the strongest among us– childbirth without even the minimum resources in totally untenable situations, juggling the care of very young children with the need to work to supplement the family's meager income, being uprooted time and again and having to learn new languages and cultures in order to survive, as well as the loneliness of being an outsider when everyone else seems to fit in. Without sugar coating these dire situations, Clene sees and appreciates God's gracious provision time and again when she had nothing left to give.

As Jesus said, *"In this world you will have trouble. But take heart! I have overcome the world."* John 16:33b This book will encourage your faith and challenge you to reach beyond any limitations to become everything that God has created you to be!

Cathy Baldizón,
Life Coach and Minister to Women

Foreword

Many voices are heard claiming that they find it impossible to reconcile the "goodness of God" with the horrors of human suffering. Those who raise this objection to the life of faith often do so in abstract philosophical categories. If you have ever struggled to "find God" in a difficult situation, you must hear Clene's story as she tells it in this moving personal account. The author is Rwandese and as a young mother and wife, she lived through the horrors of the genocide of 1994 -- horrors that are unimaginable to most. She adds her story to those other amazing souls who passed through and experienced those terrible moments and are moved to share their personal stories. But Clene's story is stunningly different. Hers is a story which testifies to the greatness of God in her own life during and after that dark period. Clene says, "Whenever I begin telling this story, I am almost speechless, as I cannot find the proper terms to describe God's greatness, faithfulness, love and compassion to me." But the Spirit gives her words that are more than adequate. They are deeply moving. Why remember and relive such terrible memories? The author has many compelling reasons. She writes,"I want to provide encouragement for women who have gone through difficult experiences, especially in the context of war. They need to know that God is still concerned about them."

She writes to offer hope to women (and men!) everywhere. To women, Clene writes, "I am completely sure that our Lord is not only aware of our vulnerability but He also has a great role for us in the building of a better society today. So let us not be lost in our misery, He is ready to do something if we are willing to let Him have first place in our lives."

This is not a story of bitterness and despair. It radiates faith, hope and gratitude. Hear Clene say, "I look at myself as the recipient of God's favour and as a testimony of what He can do performing extraordinary things through an ordinary person like you or me."

Clene's story is also a challenge to those who watch the suffering of others from a distance. It is an appeal for society to take care of those who have been hurt.

Most amazing to me is that Clene has allowed God use her season of fear and sorrow to shape a woman of unassailable faith in God's goodness. She has a sense of being "called" to share this story because through her agony she has found God in profound and unshakeable depths.

In this marvellous testimony Clene testifies, "It is time we learn that our protection, our provision and our defence comes from the Lord. It does not matter what situation we are in, our problems will never exhaust God's provision." She testifies to miracle after miracle that she herself has experienced—unexpected provision throughout her educational journey, receiving a husband given by God, shelter amidst her horrific, the birth of her firstborn amidst war and terror. There are many more.

Clene writes because she believes that "whenever God blesses us He also wants to bless other people through us. It is a promise that He gave to Abraham when He called him." So in this book she is fulfilling a divine calling.

Can God be trusted as "good" amidst the horrors of suffering? This is a voice that rings with deep confidence. Read her story and listen as she bears witness that "through suffering everything is made new: new foundations, new expectations and longings, new fulfilments, new ways of thinking...Through suffering I received assurance that the God of my salvation and confidence cares about me."

Her family was prophetic in giving her the name 'Nyiramahoro' which means 'the giver or owner of peace'.

George Renner, PhD
Director, Institute for the Study of African Realities
NEGST
Nairobi, Kenya

Preface

A number of books have been written about the 1994 Rwandan tragedy. Many of those have described the events as they took place and the political situation at that moment. There has been very little written, however, about how God intervened in the midst of death, fear and sorrow to protect and to provide. It is very important for the people who passed through and experienced those terrible moments to offer their personal stories which testify to the greatness of God in their lives during and after that dark period. Of course, some stories have been told and written as second hand information. Mine is one of those that has gone untold until now.

Through writing this book I want to provide encouragement for women who have gone through difficult experiences, especially in the context of war. They need to know that God is still concerned about them. Some may have lost their children and husbands and be left all by themselves. Others may have lost their property, jobs or businesses and do not know how to continue supporting their families. Others may have lost their identity and dignity. They find themselves feeling useless and hopeless. They have become victims of the collapse of structures and initiatives for democracy, peace and justice, human rights abuse, reconciliation and leadership. But God is still in control and is very much concerned with every single aspect of their lives.

In the Bible we see the story of Naomi who after losing her husband and her two sons, was redeemed by the Lord in the most unexpected way. God used a Gentile woman, her daughter-in-law, Ruth, to restore Naomi's honour, identity and dignity. Ruth's story is very encouraging. We are reminded that our destiny is in God's hand. In our society, especially in Africa, we have been taught to believe that without men in our lives we are useless. This way of thinking has put many girls and women into very vulnerable situations and has allowed wicked men to take advantage and abuse them. It is time we learn that our protection, our provision and our defence comes from the Lord. It does not matter what situation we are in, our problems will never exhaust God's provision. When we surrender totally and completely to Him, He takes care of us, He wipes our tears and heals our hearts.

I also want to make an appeal for society to take care of those who have been hurt. They need help. They need people they can trust and to whom they can pour out their hearts. Many women need to talk and cry as a means of bringing relief for their pain. Give them this opportunity.

War is the most devastating thing I have ever seen. Only when you have experienced it can you really understand its destructive effects on people. I have come a long way to reach the place where I am today. Many people came into my life and encouraged me and helped me to see that all was not lost. I know how much I was affected as a young mother and wife, and I am sure there are many other women today -- in Rwanda, across Africa and around the world -- who are still in the bondage of despair. Let us be part of healing the wounded hearts around us. Let us be sensitive to those who are grieving. If you have been affected in one way or another and you have been able to overcome, do not keep quiet. There is someone who needs to hear your story and hope for victory. Conversely, perhaps there is someone who is totally unaware of what women in crisis situations are going through and is just waiting for a story that touches her heart so that she can be part of the peace building process.

Women, I am completely sure that our Lord is not only aware of our vulnerability but He also has a great role for us in the building of a better society today. So let us not be lost in our misery, He is ready to do something if we are willing to let Him have first place in our lives.

My prayer is for every woman who will read this book to be encouraged knowing that Jesus is the only one who can give us victory. He does not, however, work in a vacuum. He works through people. Are we going to collaborate with Him? Are we willing to let Him change our lives and our society in general? Are we willing to let ourselves be empowered by Him? I would be happy to collaborate with you and be part of what you are doing. I am available to anyone who wants to use the knowledge that has been imparted to me in order to change society for better.

May God bless you!

Clene

The Butterfly's Lesson

"One day, a small opening appeared in a cocoon and a man sat and watched the butterfly for several hours as it struggled to force its body through that little hole.

Then, it seems to stop making any progress. It appeared as if it had gotten as far as it could and it could not go any further.

So the man decided to help the butterfly: he took a pair of scissors and opened the cocoon.

The butterfly then emerged easily.

But it had a tiny, withered body and shrivelled wings.

The man continued to watch expecting that at any moment the wings would open, enlarge, expand and become firm, to be able to support the butterfly's body.

But nothing happened! In fact, the butterfly spent the rest of its short life crawling around with a withered body and shrivelled wings. It was never able to fly.

What the man in his kindness and goodwill did not understand was that the restricting cocoon and the struggle required for the butterfly to get through the tiny opening, are God's way of forcing fluid from the body of the butterfly into its wings, so that it can be ready for flight once it achieves freedom from the cocoon.

Sometimes, struggles are exactly what we need in our life.

If God allowed us to go through our life without any obstacles, it would cripple us. We would not be as strong as we could have been and never be able to fly.

Anonymous

JOURNEY INTO LIFE

"I knew you before I formed you in your mother's womb. Before you were born I set you apart and appointed you as my spokesman to the world."

Jeremiah 1:5

My life began in Rurenge, a remote village in the Eastern Province of Rwanda, on June 29, 1965. I was fourth in a family of nine and had four sisters and four brothers. At that time only about 50 families lived in the village. The main economic activity was farming and hunting was practiced as well. June is normally a very hot month, with temperatures rising to 30 degrees and it is the time to harvest sorghum, beans, and maize. Harvest time was a fun time. After bringing the grain in from the fields at around 11 a.m., people would gather in one of the homes to have a drink and share the roasted maize.

When I was growing up, communal life was part of the culture. Different families would come together to do their work in a group. They spent a day or two harvesting one person's field and then would go around in a circle until all the fields had been harvested. This communal style was the norm whenever an urgent task needed to be done such as sowing, weeding or harvesting, or in case of fire to help rebuild a neighbour's hut. This lifestyle gave us all a sense of belonging.

I never asked my mother what happened when I was born, but based on what I saw in other cases I imagine that when she had me the women in the village gathered at my father's home to help harvest the grains from our field. Of course having a new born was extra special and there definitely would be a celebration with the naming ceremony to follow. According to my mother, prior to my birth, my parents had had some disagreements with my grandfather. So my grandfather had said that they would not have another child. But when my mother conceived and eventually gave birth, my grandfather came and declared peace upon my father's house. They were grateful and as a way of showing that they had received the peace, they called me 'Nyiramahoro' which means 'the giver or owner of peace'. And my brother who came after me was called 'Mahoro' which simply means 'peace.'

We had plenty of food in our home because my mother was a hard-working woman and she took care of the farm. In addition, the land we occupied was recently deforested and therefore still very fertile. Additionally at that time there were still people who hunted as their way of life. Because my father was among the few people who knew how to read, he was very well respected in the village. On every hunting day, we knew our family was going to get the nicest part of the meat before the hunters would share their meat with everyone else.

My father was a primary school teacher and everyone called him "Mwalimu" which means "teacher" because he was the only teacher originating from the village, and almost everyone who went to school had to pass through his class. In fact many of the people who sent their children to school at that time did so because of him. Most people knew very little about education. Going to school was considered a waste of time for many.

My father was a class one teacher. There was no pre-primary school at that time. He took me to school a bit early, probably as a way of reducing the work-load for my mother. I did not know why I had to go to school. It was three kilometres away from home. I had to go with my sister and brother and was not able to keep up with their speed. With my heavy body, I had to go running after them. By the time we reached school I was always exhausted. You cannot imagine the trauma I had to go through as a young girl. It was hard for me to wake up early and walk three kilometres to school barefoot. Many times, I was found sleeping in class and my father would not care about my age but would beat me bitterly. I was so disappointed and hated school. Sometimes I would pretend to be sick as a way of escaping, but my parents would not give in.

For the whole of my lower primary courses, my performance was very poor. But God had planned a way to change that situation by strategically taking me away from my family environment. I did not realize what was happening at that time. Many times we do not realize that God is at work in our lives and He does not need to involve us, but it is important to understand that no matter what happens to us, God knows the reason for it.

I am sure that when Ruth decided to follow her mother-in-law to the foreign land she did not expect to become a great woman who was going to be remembered forever. She did not care about possible discrimination that she was going to face, living a life of want. Elimelech and his family's resettlement to Moab ended in tragedy but it also fit well into the strategic, redemptive plan of God.

In 1974, one of my uncles took me away from home. He was working in a school in a village called Shyira in western Rwanda, almost 200 km from my home village. He was still single and wanted two children to live with him. In my culture, at least during that time, you could not live alone unless something was seriously wrong with you. Children belong to the community not just to their biological father and mother and a paternal uncle is actually like your own father. So what he did was perfectly in order for our culture. He chose my younger brother and me. I was very happy because at that time a number of good things took place. For the first time I was provided with slippers (not even shoes), and I was going to travel by bus. For the first time I was going to see the Rwandan capital city of Kigali and I would see electricity and different kinds of buildings. For the first time, I saw water taps and many other things that I had not seen in my village.

Because my uncle was working in a mission school, his house was not far from the church building. For the first time I was introduced to Sunday school and I enjoyed it very much. The small local church we attended when I was still in my village had never had Sunday school for children. There was only one service, and when it was time to preach, they told all the children to go outside. It was fun but not helpful in terms of our Christian growth. My uncle was not necessarily a committed Christian but encouraged me to be in the church. It was so exciting to be with the other children and to sing those Sunday school songs. My favourite was a chorus composed from Mark 10:13-15. I felt so special and enjoyed being in the church and learning more about Jesus who loved small children.

My uncle took me to a new school. The school was beautiful compared to where I was coming from. It was built with strong red bricks, it had glass windows (though most of them were broken), and it had better classrooms with more comfortable desks. It also seemed the school had teachers with better qualifications than those from my home area. They had so many books. Every year a number of students from that school qualified and were selected for secondary education.

After the first test my uncle realized how poor my performance was and he decided to work with me seriously to bring my education up to his standards. Every evening, I had an assignment, especially in French. He made me understand that if I could not do well in school, I had no future. His idea stuck in my mind and fear took hold of me, as I was aware that I was not doing well in school. In class, I was frustrated because I found myself far behind compared to my new classmates. I began working hard on my French but I eventually had to repeat class five before I could go to class six after which I was supposed to sit for the national exams. By the end of my class five, I was among the best pupils of the school. That foundation helped me to successfully complete high school and later go to university. I was glad to have had someone make a positive impact in my life and to this day I respect and appreciate my uncle for that.

LAYING FOUNDATIONS

*"Be very careful never to forget what you have seen the
Lord do for you. Do not let these things escape from
your mind as long as you live. And be sure to pass them
on to your children and grandchildren."*

Deuteronomy 4:9

Having been with my uncle whose ambition was to go as high as he could in education, I took him as a model. I felt I was accountable to him as far as education was concerned, and I did not want to disappoint him. I was determined and because of that I was able to go higher in education than my siblings, even though I was not the most intelligent person in the family. I am convinced that the encouragement I received from my uncle contributed to my success in school. He created in me the desire to learn and to aim higher. He believed in what I was able to achieve and he encouraged me to go for that. Unconsciously he fulfilled God's command to His people by teaching me and passing on to me what he believed was best for my future. God used him to prepare and set me on the path that God wanted me to follow. The culture of failure in my father's house was broken. My three older siblings had not been able to successfully go through high school but all my younger siblings were able to at least complete high school and three of them are now degree holders.

Whenever God blesses us He also wants to bless other people through us. It is a promise that He gave to Abraham when He called him. He said,

"I will bless you and make you famous, and I will make you a blessing to others." Genesis 12:2

When I see where I come from I can declare without doubt that this has been true in my own life. I remember my matron of honour telling her daughter just prior to my wedding that she should look at me as a model. I look at myself as the recipient of God's favour and as a testimony of what He can do performing extraordinary things through an ordinary person like you or me.

Now I can say along with the psalmist that

> *"Your favour, o Lord, made me as secure as the*
> *mountain"* Psalm 30:7.

But the fact that God is at work in our lives does not necessarily mean that we are free from opposition, disappointment and discouragement. When those giants are in our way we just need to face them like David did,

> *"You come to me with sword, spear and javelin, but*
> *I come to you in the name of the Lord Almighty."*
> 1Samuel 17:45

It was amazing how every time when I was ready to go to the next level of education, someone would come from nowhere to throw a word of discouragement at me. I remember when my father broke the news that not only had I qualified for high school, but I had also been selected to attend. (Not everyone who qualified was taken because of the limited number of schools at that time compared to the number of contestants.) I was so excited! Then my cousin who was visiting us told me, "Just go and have a look, because next year you will be back in the village with us."

She was indirectly referring to my two sisters who had gone ahead of me but were discontinued at the end of their first year due to their lack of a good educational foundation beginning in primary school, since most of the teachers in my area were not qualified. In my village only when a student reached class six would she or he have a qualified teacher (that is a teacher with some formal teacher training).

Although I had not followed in my sisters' footsteps I was fearful and sometimes I thought that I was not any more qualified than they were so it was easy to agree with my cousin's comments. But ultimately I refused to accept that and instead I was determined to prove everyone wrong who thought I was not going to make it. It was a battle that God Himself was ready to fight and I am glad He did. Not only did I successfully complete high school, but I did so with sufficiently high grades to enable me to sit for an exam to go on for post-secondary education.

Our school system was such that for the first three years of secondary there was no emphasis on any particular area of profession. After those three years, known as "Tronc Commun" when students were approximately 15 years old, there was a national examination which was meant to help the candidates go for professional training for another three or four years.

There was also the option of a short course for two years, after which you immediately went for a job for which you have been trained. With this two-year certificate, it was not possible to go to university afterwards. It happened that when the national exam results came out, I found out that I had been accepted for the two-year course. I was then supposed to go back to the same school. I spent the whole night crying as I knew it signalled the end of my education after two years' time. My uncle came to visit us and I told him about the results. When he heard the news, he actually encouraged me because that particular year many students had not been placed in any school and thus, he made it clear that I was among the lucky ones to have any chance at all. I consoled myself.

When it was time for me to go to school, I went and met a number of my high school classmates. I completed that course in June 1983 and was immediately given a teaching position. I took it without much excitement but my father was happy because I was going to help him take care of my younger siblings. I would like to say that I was also happy to do that, but I felt dissatisfaction in my heart. I wanted to contribute to my family, but I also felt bitterly disappointed at not being able to continue my education.

God, however, had not forgotten my dream. His ear was ever attentive to my cries and desires even though I did not know Him fully. That is His promise to all of us.

Before the end of my first month of teaching, I went to my former school to get my certificate because I needed to open a file as an employee. The director of the school, a Catholic nun from Belgium, told me there was a possibility for me to go back to school. It happened that the ministry of education had introduced a new system of schooling immediately after I left primary school. I did six years in primary school, but those who came after me studied for eight years in primary, then six years in secondary and after that they could go to university straight away. By the time my class finished its two year short course, the first people in the new system were still only in class three of high school. This meant that for another three years, no one would be graduating from high school. So a bridging class was introduced to incorporate people who had finished with honours from the old short course system. I immediately applied and the following week I received an acceptance letter.

Elated at this unexpected opportunity, I left my teaching job and went back to school for yet another certificate course of study. My father was not happy with this development, but again my uncle was able to convince him. I completed these additional three years in 1986. My father was excited because he thought that this time around I was done with my studies and that with the new certificate I would earn a slightly higher salary. However, that was not my objective -- I knew the new certificate would give me access to university. I had applied even before I had finished the certificate courses. So, in September 1986, I was admitted to the National University of Rwanda. It was like a dream to my father and a surprise to many. As the writer of the book of Proverbs says,

"Hope deferred makes the heart sick, but when dreams come true, there is life and joy." Proverbs 13:12

By then I knew what I thought was impossible was definitely becoming a reality.

In Rwandan culture in the 1980's, it was believed that once a girl went to university, she would lose her moral status. That was one of my father's primary concerns. I assured him that I was not like any other girl, that I knew what I was looking for and that I was going only for an education. Of course, that did not mean that I was not insecure. I myself wondered how I was going to keep the moral standard that my parents expected. But I had some confidence —although I was a young believer, I knew my Christian faith was my infallible protection. I knew my God was going to be with me and I enjoyed the companionship of God for the six years I spent at the university. Words that were given to Isaiah became mine,

"Fear not for I have redeemed you, I have summoned you by name, you are mine. When you pass through the waters, I will be with you, and when you pass through the rivers they will not sweep over you. When you walk through the fire you will not be burned, the flames will not set you ablaze." Isaiah 43:1-3

Additionally for the first time my father was not going to have to pay for my fees, since I immediately got a government scholarship.

Going to university was very rare in Rwanda at that time, especially if you were a girl, for the value of a girl depended on the kind of man she married. In fact, my parents had to answer questions like "How can you allow your daughter to go to University?" and "Who is going to marry her after she gets old?" and "What is she looking for, getting a husband is the highest achievement a girl should aim for", and so on. These questions increased my father's anxiety even more, but he knew I was determined. He gave me his blessing and I left. He wanted to escort me to university, which was about 200 km from my home, but I told him I was now old enough to take care of myself. I did not want to bother him anymore. I was very sure once I got to the bus station I would meet other students and that way I would not be alone. Still the venture was very scary and I was not sure what to expect. However, God had His own way and He provided for all my needs.

MY TIME AT THE UNIVERSITY

"For the Lord Almighty has purposed and who can thwart him? His hand is stretched out, and who can turn it back?" Isaiah 14:27

The year 1986 marked the beginning of my life at the university. It was like a dream. I was not sure I was going to make it because the system was so rigid and only the smartest people could advance. Nevertheless, my joy was that even if I did not finish, at least my name would appear in the record of those who once attended the university. That was also a source of pride for me coming from a place where very few people completed primary school.

I was assigned to study Geography and History. There were four girls in that class and twenty men. The first day after registration, we were reading the notice board, when a young man approached us and asked what we had come to study. We said Geography and History. He replied sarcastically, "People who study Geography are mad people -- do you want to be mad?" I do not remember the answer we gave him, but that was only adding to the pressure and fear, which were already abundant. The first week was a week of orientation and professors from different departments were speaking to us. The French they spoke impressed me, most of them had done their studies in France. I started wondering whether I would be able to follow them once the classes began.

At the end of the first week, there was a student riot. Apparently they did not like the Vice Rector of the campus. We were forced out of our rooms and told to support the riot without even knowing what it was all about. For two weeks, we did not have classes and we spent time attending meetings led by the students who organized the riot and each time we were assigned different duties to discharge. Failure to take care of your duty could result in severe punishment. It was the first disappointment in our lives on campus.

My time at the university, however, was also a time of spiritual awakening, awareness and growth. During my childhood, I had had a very shallow faith, not really understanding what being a Christian meant. For my seven years of high school, I was in a Catholic school. I had admired the Belgian sisters who ran the school. I had been taught to be a prayerful girl, I had learned to recite the rosary but because I came from a Protestant background, I was confused as to who was most important - Jesus or Mary, His mother. For the first year at university, I attended charismatic group fellowships for Catholics as well as Protestant prayer groups. I am grateful for my colleagues, members of GBU (Groupe Biblique Universitaire), who really took care of me and helped me forge a deeper faith. I think my salvation was renewed and I began to appreciate the lives of young people who were saved. I looked at them as real brothers and sisters. Their fellowship helped me to grow and offered me protection in the secular environment of the university.

My values slowly began to change. Up until then, I had held education as my highest life goal. I began to understand that important people are not necessarily those who hold big academic degrees, but instead those who fear God. A degree can guarantee a job and profession but it cannot guarantee a better and purposeful life or salvation. So although I continued to look forward to having my degree, I began making growth in faith a priority. I carefully chose the places where I wanted to be and avoided any environment which could lead me into temptation.

I made it a point not to go to the cinema because of the kind of movies (mostly pornographic) that were shown. I avoided most parties, which of course always involved a lot of drinking and dancing.

I learnt how to choose new friends and how to interact with them depending on whether there were saved or not. Having male friends in my life who were not saved was excluded. For the scripture says,

> *"If one falls down, his friends can help him up. But*
> *pity is a man who falls and has no one to help him."*
> Ecclesiastes 4:10

I was determined that if I was to get married, the essential factor I was looking for in my future husband was his faith in Christ.

AFTER THE UNIVERSITY

"There is within my heart a melody
Jesus whispers and low
Fear not, I am with thee, peace be still,
In all of life's ebb and flow."[1]

In 1992, when I graduated from the National University of Rwanda with a degree in Geography, I thought it was the beginning of a good and comfortable life. To complete my imagined ideal life, I had a number of longings. First, I longed to have significance and a positive impact. This, I thought, was going to happen by getting a good job and earning enough money. Taking care of my parents who had sacrificed for years to pay my fees was my greatest excitement. But this did not happen.

During that time one did not apply for jobs. After graduation, people waited to be posted. I approached the people I knew whom I believed had the power to get me a good job or at least recommend me for one. It did not work so quickly and yet I needed money. Meanwhile the ministry of education posted me and I was given a teaching job at Gahini high school. Gahini, for those who remember the history of the East African Revival in the 1930s, is a village situated in the Eastern Province of Rwanda where the Revival started before spreading to Uganda, Kenya and Tanzania. The appointment was announced via the radio. Not only didn't I want a teaching job but I also did not want to go to Gahini, but of course refusing a government job could result in some serious sanctions. Gahini was almost 100 km from my home and there were no proper communication facilities available.

At the same time I learned that in my home town another school was looking for a French teacher. It would be convenient for me to work there since my brother worked at that school as an accountant and at least I was sure of proper accommodations and free food until I could get my salary. When I approached the principal of the school he gave me the offer which I gladly accepted and I was sure I was only going to be there for a short time. The principal was to write a letter explaining the reasons why I did not go to Gahini.

Meanwhile I was still hoping to get the job of my dreams. I did not even ask God for it because I believed so much in myself and in people who had promised to help. Fortunately He had not given up on me and He was still dealing with me in His own way. The pride that was setting in was definitely dangerous and many young people fall into this trap. In our societies where very few people make it to live a better life it is very easy to get disoriented and lose our focus. But God in His own wisdom closes all those doors that we sometimes try very hard to have open to us so that we turn back to Him. At the end of the day it is not about our qualifications, it is about God's purpose for our lives. We need to be sensitive to His calling and be willing to follow in obedience.

At that time I was 27 years old. My mother was worried because according to the culture I should already be married but this was not a priority for me at that time. My younger sisters were by then finishing their high school and soon were going to get married. Culturally, if my younger sisters got married before me, it would be a disaster. I started feeling pressure but I was not worried. I only needed to be sure that I was financially settled. But that never happened. The job I had hoped for never materialized; my teaching job paid very little, and even then it took quite a while for a newly employed teacher to be put on the payroll. A file needed to be completed first and since I had just graduated I needed to wait several months for my certificates to come out.

Additionally the political situation in the country was getting worse. Even the towns were having problems with water and electricity. Many businesses were closing down because of lack of electricity and security. Everyone was preoccupied trying to get the basic commodities and the security situation was becoming threatening. The number of displaced people from the north-western part of the country was increasing and although I didn't know it then, my husband-to-be joined the ranks of the displaced in 1990. The level of poverty was alarming and many young people without any source of income were taking advantage of the situation. Robbery and looting were frequent.

Everyone started worrying about personal safety and I actually started to appreciate the job I had. A number of infrastructures had already been damaged by war. It was hard to see where the country was going and it was becoming obvious that dark days were setting in. No one knew where the solution to our problems would come from. There were so many prophets, Christians were praying and in many cases God revealed what was about to happen. Repentance messages were preached. But as usual only those who have divine revelation take prophecies seriously. There were also messages from visionary people. Confusion was slowly overtaking. We only hoped that the political conflicts would come to an end. Some areas of the country were relatively safer than others depending on how far or close they were from the areas where fighting between government soldiers and the Rwandan Patriot Front (RPF) forces were taking place. I had no other choice than to continue teaching until I met my husband to be in January 1993.

HOW I MET MY HUSBAND

"God's joy will be yours if you choose His best"[2]

I had been attending an educational seminar at a neighbouring school and in the cool evening I was walking to my residence with a number of colleagues. Some women were selling pineapples on the side of the road so we decided to have some. While we were there three people on motorcycle came by and stopped to greet us. One of my colleagues was with two strangers, Deo, and a friend of his. They behaved as if they knew all of us. When our colleague introduced them to us he specifically pointed at me and said these two fellows had come to see me. I thought he was joking and did not take him seriously. I said that if they had come to see me, they should come back another time. With an affirmative nod of the head and a very subtle smile, Deo said they would be coming back.

How did he know me? Apparently he had seen me at one of the Christian Union camps which we held every Christmas holiday. And we had also met at the wedding of one of my friends who happened to be his relative, but in both instances I never noticed him. Coincidentally he had been appointed the chaplain and dean of students at Gahini. So when he heard on the radio that I was to be posted to Gahini, in his heart he was convinced that I was the one he was going to marry. When I did not report to the Gahini School he decided to find out where I had gone and when we met he was actually on his search tour. I remember he was wearing a heavy brown sweater with a small cross on it. He looked very calm and I had the impression that he was a Catholic brother, since that is how many of them behaved.

In the same month, their school football team had a match to play against our school team. He had to accompany the team since he was in charge of student affairs including sports. That was his opportunity to come back. He showed up at the place where I was living with my brother and found us playing Scrabble with some other colleagues. No one paid any attention to him, not even me. I thought he was looking for my colleague whom he had been with on the previous visit. When he realized that nothing was happening from my side, he took his friend aside and asked him to tell me that he wanted to talk with me. I was surprised and wondered what it was that he wanted to tell me.

I took him to our house and now he introduced himself properly to me. The thing that impressed me was the fact he was a pastor. And of course he was very smart. He told me how God convinced him after hearing my name that I was the one he was supposed to marry. Hard to believe - in fact I was shocked. He said he was giving me time to think about it and he was planning to come back another day. I did not know what to say or to tell my brother. Actually my brother was wondering what business I had to talk about with that pastor. But in my heart I knew something was happening. On the next visit he asked if it was possible to visit my family at home. I said fine. So I went home and told my parents. My brother was not interested. My sisters were and those who were married actually came home to meet him. The younger one was still in school. My father was happy to receive him. When he left my father was wondering whether there was any relationship between me and that pastor. I told my father that he was interested in me. Then he said that that was the kind of son-in-law he would like to have. In my heart I said "wow"!

I still had a battle within myself but the more I saw and interacted with Deo, the more I became convinced that he was the one God wanted me to marry. Whenever I shared about him with my friends and colleagues many of them thought I was crazy. They made funny comments which did not matter to me. I was determined. In June 1993, we were officially engaged. I did not think anymore about the many opportunities that I was hoping to get. In fact I later learned that a company which wanted to hire me looked for me and didn't know my contacts so the job was given to someone else. One of my professors who was associated with the company had also promised to facilitate my access to the doctoral program in Geography. But he also couldn't trace me. We later met during the week of my wedding and he couldn't believe I was giving up that opportunity. But later I understood that God had a different plan for me, a plan to fully serve Him, and He needed to give me a partner who would support me in that. I have to agree with Dr. Muindi that,

"God does not call us to all people but he does place specific ones along our paths for relationship and ministry."[3]

Though many questions were not answered in my heart, that decision clearly marked the beginning of my journey into full time service for the Lord. I had no idea how it was going to happen but God did and here I am. I did not know what to expect, but I knew challenges were ahead as I married a displaced person, without a home who was struggling to survive. But that was good preparation for the kind of life many of us were about to begin and of which we were unaware.

Pastors were considered unworthy marriage partners for university-educated women. They did not have a good salary; they couldn't afford a comfortable life, which many people believed could only be attained through university education and big jobs. But there was one truth that I have learned: true comfort comes from knowing the Lord. As the scripture says,

"Better a little with the fear of the Lord than great wealth with turmoil." Proverbs 15:16

I remember one of my aunts who categorically refused to attend my wedding. Paternal aunts were very important people when it came to girls' weddings. She was the one to initiate me to the new life I was about to begin, give me proper instructions about how to become a good wife and a mother. Unfortunately she missed that opportunity. It was painful to me, but I forgave her. I only pray that she may know personally the God that we serve who is the giver of real peace, joy and prosperity. I constantly pray that the Lord may redeem her life and her children's lives.

I have learned that my real relatives are those who do the will of God. Those who live a life without Christ are hopeless. When I received the message that my aunt was not going to come, God provided another option, a better one. My parents talked to a sister in Christ called Felicita and asked her to take my aunt's place. She was the daughter of my late godmother. She was a committed Christian and I will never forget the last night before my wedding in my father's house when she came and spent time with me praying and praising God, encouraging me and giving me the assurance that though the journey I was about to begin was very hard, the Lord would always go with me. She said I had nothing to fear. The time I spent with Felicita ended up being more precious than the counsel or gifts that I would have expected to get from my aunt. This reminds me of when Jesus' parents came looking for Him and found Him in the Temple courts, sitting among the teachers. When He was asked why He did not go with them his answer was,

"Did you not know I had to be in my Father's house?"
Luke 2:49

Again this was preparing me for the life ahead, where for many years I would not live with my real relatives but God would give me so many other siblings, friends and parents in the Lord. Indeed in my journey I have learned that there is nothing more precious than being close to godly people and being busy in the things of God.

How we began our family

"Unless the Lord builds the house, its builders labour in vain". Psalm 127:1

My husband and I were married August 28, 1993 which marked the beginning of a new chapter in my life. I immediately joined him to work at the Gahini High School. How interesting that some months before I had been posted to that school and refused to go. The ways of the Lord are sometimes ironic. No matter how hard we plan our ways if they do not fit into God's plan they will never come to pass.

At that time the people of his area, including his parents and siblings, were already displaced because of the war. He had a very heavy responsibility to take care of the whole family, since he was the only one working. A number of his siblings were already living with us in the same house. He had to rent an extra house for his parents and one of his sisters and her family but his salary couldn't cater for all those expenses. When we got married things were not necessarily better, because now even our two salaries were not sufficient. You can imagine beginning a family in that kind of setting! From the beginning of our marriage it was clear that things were not going to be easy. I, however, tried to dismiss the thoughts and pretend that it would all be ok. Since I had not directly experienced the effects of the war I had very little understanding of what displaced people were going through. Soon I would learn first hand.

Our honeymoon was spent right in our house. During that period there were many children from the displaced families who were not able to go to school. The Episcopoal Church in Rwanda, Byumba diocese, decided to begin a school to accommodate them.

They needed an educated and trained pastor to take on the responsibility of the school. Since my husband was among the few who held a degree, and given that he himself had been affected by the war, they thought he suited the post. They also thought the two of us constituted a good team to be able to set up a school. After consultation among the bishops, it was decided that we should move to the new school. This was a big challenge to us as we had only been married for two months.

So many transitions were taking place at the same time. We

experienced many disappointments along with much excitement mixed with fear, of course. We were happy with the appointment, because just looking at those displaced children and seeing how glad they were to be able to learn was something to rejoice in. Initially there were just three of us, my husband, the secretary, and me. I felt fulfilled for I highly valued what I was doing. I not only did the school work of teaching and helping with the correspondence that needed to be dealt with, but also whenever there were visitors such as various partners of the church, I was the hostess since there were no hotels or restaurants. That of course added to our expenses but by growing vegetables and keeping rabbits, the load was much easier and I enjoyed doing it.

The school was located in a remote area in Byumba diocese, where there was no electricity or running water. Displaced people living in miserable conditions and depending on UNHCR insufficient food distributions surrounded us. I was so sympathetic. We did not have enough food ourselves but at least we had a shelter. We started thinking about how we could help them.

I remember one particular family whose small hut was close to the fence of our house. She had small children and I could hear them crying all the time from hunger. It was very unsettling. I begged the vicar of the parish which hosted the school to give me a small piece of land so that I could grow some food. He said the Parish did not have enough land so was not able to help. But finally he agreed to give me about 30 square meters close to my house. It was small but I was able to grow some vegetables. The neighbouring family took care of the garden.

My garden did so well that people in the area were surprised. Some of them had never seen vegetables like carrots, lettuces and courgettes, also called zucchini. They often came to ask me what I had planted in my garden. I was reminded of what God said through the prophet Isaiah: *"He will also send you rain for the seed you sow in the ground, and the food that comes from the land will be rich and plentiful."* Isaiah 30:23

It felt good to wake up and look at my garden and see how my gardener's family was happy because now they could get some money and vegetables every week. This gave us a new idea. Since our school was not doing well financially, we thought that if we planted more vegetables we could have enough for our students and sell the rest in order to get money to cover some of the other expenses. I was given responsibility for the project. Together with the teachers and students we decided to work on the land that was given to the school and we planted vegetables. Unfortunately when they were almost ready for harvest, the war had spread so that we all had to leave. Months later I met a lady who had not been able to flee and was left hiding there. She told me that after everyone else was gone the few people who were left behind lived on the carrots that we left ripening in the field. I was so happy because again I could see that whatever we do is not for our own sake but God's. And this was Paul's reminder,

"...be strong and steady, always enthusiastic about the Lord's work, for you know that nothing you do for the Lord is ever useless" 1Corinthians 15:58 - New Living Translation

We did not benefit directly from what we planted but someone else did. And at the same time God had put people at our end who were ready to feed us and take care of our needs. Our God, who is so loving, plans ahead of us and His plans are always the best. As Jesus says:

> *"Look at the birds of the air; they do not sow or reap*
> *or store away in barns and yet your heavenly father*
> *feeds them. Are you not much valuable that they?"*
> Matthew 6:26

WHEN ALL YOUR FOUNDATIONS ARE SHAKEN

"For no other foundation can anyone lay than
that which is laid, which is Jesus Christ."
1 Corinthians 3:11

"If anyone among you seems to be wise in this age,
let him become a fool that he may become wise. For
the wisdom of this world is foolishness with God"
1 Corinthians 3:18

On Wednesday morning, April 6, unexpected news reached us. The presidential jet had been blown up. Communication was cut. There was general confusion. No one seemed to know what was happening or what was going to happen, but rumours were flying everywhere.

By then I was nine months pregnant with my first child. There were no good hospitals around and the small clinic that was available was closed because no one was at work. I wished I would give birth to my baby quickly. I did not even know how childbirth happens and there was no one around to instruct me. Fear of the unknown and the unrest became so great that no one was able to eat or sleep. This was affecting my baby; I began to realize that the movements of the baby were irregular. I asked my husband to get someone who could take me to one of the best hospitals in the region, the Gahini mission hospital. Someone with a pick-up truck offered to take me. It was a two hour drive from what was then our home. I had a suitcase with some of the clothes for my baby so I took it along with another one, which had things that were not often used. Those were not the things that I needed necessarily but I did not have time to sort them out. I also had an idea that it would be good to carry some of my husband's clothes. Without asking him, I took two of his suits and two shirts. He found me packing them and he almost took them out of the suitcase. I told him not to bother because when I came back I would bring them with me anyway. So he agreed. This turned out to be providential, as these clothes in the suitcases ended up being the only items from our home that we had with us during several months' flight from the war.

My husband escorted me on the long drive to the hospital and then went back home. The plan was for me to wait at my sister-in-law's house not far from the hospital for my baby to be ready to be born.

The next morning when we woke up, my husband was standing at the door knocking. The people were fleeing the area because of the approaching gunfire. The need to flee was so urgent that he had run away in pyjamas and carrying nothing else. He said he was in such turmoil that he had even left behind a fairly large sum of money (that was meant to buy food for the students); he simply did not remember to grab it in his haste.

A few minutes later, our whole household was there. Students and staff from the school we were responsible for and everybody who was living in our house joined us. Other members of the family also followed. The sister's house became too small to accommodate all of us. Some were taken to the student dormitories in a Secondary School where my husband had worked before we got married. Most secondary schools in Rwanda are boarding schools and since schools were on vacation, dormitories were being used to house the many people who were displaced.

People continued flowing in. We stayed indoors because of fear. The noise of heavy arms was obvious and was getting closer. People around us were fleeing – on the move again. I told my husband that if we did not go with the others I might die because I was not going to be able to walk fast if the fighting happened to begin in that area. All of a sudden we saw the director of the school that was accommodating us packing things in the school pick-up. I told my husband "Look, those people are going and we must go with them because they have a car." We did not have time to negotiate we just threw our two suitcases in and immediately took off. That was the beginning of a long journey full of anxiety.

On the way, my purse and the small bag that had all our important papers, including our academic and marriage certificates fell out of the car. We asked the person who was driving the car to stop so we might pick it. He stopped and my husband got out of the car to pick up the suitcase and my purse. Fearing for her life, the director's wife who was sitting next to me said that they should not wait for him because he was putting them in danger. I told them that if they were going to leave my husband behind I was going to be left, too. Thank God, the director did not heed his wife's panicked advice. They waited for him.

After a few minutes, my husband came back with the suitcase, but without my purse. This proved tragic, as my purse contained my identity card and the only money we had. During that time, being without an ID was criminal and enough to warrant death. My life was then left in God's hands. Still that was not my biggest concern, for I was constantly thinking of my unborn baby and the impending delivery. Evening came. We began thinking of possible places where we could spend the night. Things had changed and people had changed too. It did not matter whether you knew a person before; trust was gone. Everyone was full of fear and suspicion. We tried knocking at a number of doors where we thought people knew us, including one school in which I had taught before but we were denied access. This reminded me of Joseph and Mary as they were looking for a place where they could have their baby and no one was willing to give them a place to sleep.

We had no choice but to continue searching. We continued towards my hometown where my brother and a number of friends lived. Road blocks were so frequent that it took more than two hours to cover less than 2 km. We managed to get into a church compound and the bishop welcomed us into his home where we stayed indoors for three days.

The next day, our students from the school where we had been working arrived and my husband felt a duty to look for a place for them. He went to the school where my brother worked and where I had worked before I got married.

Since our students were given permission to stay on the school premises where my brother worked, we also went with them in order to leave room for more and more people who were still flowing into the bishop's house. That evening we learned that the school had also given accommodation to some personnel from the Red Cross and Doctors Without Borders. I told my husband to go to the medical workers to see if he could get anything that would help us when the baby came, because by then it was very clear that the delivery was not going to be in a hospital. He went and fortunately he met a young man who was working with Doctors Without Borders (a medical agency). My husband explained our situation to him and he told him that they had lost all their equipment and drugs as they fled but agreed to check and see if there was anything at all that he could give us.

He returned with a few vitamin K tablets and said, "This is the only thing I have."

My husband took them in faith without even asking how these tablets would be helpful. The young man urged us to go and buy a new razor blade and a needle, which we did. Many questions were filling my mind, such as, "Is this really what I need to have a safe delivery and a safe baby? Am I going to make it?" I wanted to dismiss them from my mind, but I was unable to do that.

Before 7 a.m. the next morning we heard the rumble of heavy arms in town. Confusion reigned again. We had previously agreed that if we were to leave that place we would go with my brother. We could not find him. Since we were in a car which was not our own, we could not wait for him. We later learnt that he had boarded one of the Red Cross trucks and had been able to leave town safely. We begged the Red Cross to carry our students also.

As for us, things continued to be very complicated. That was the beginning of a most difficult trip because we were heading to regions where people did not know us. The insecurity was horrible. We managed to reach another church which was only 20 km from the town where we had parted with my brother. We found shelter in a primary school classroom and used some benches as beds. It was getting more and more difficult to find anything to eat since we had no money to buy food, firewood or water. However, we were so anxious that we were not even hungry much of the time.

In fact, I was feeling so anxious that almost nothing mattered.

We spent two days at that church. By the third day, bombs and artillery were heard again, and fleeing crowds of people continued flowing past. We knew it was time to move again. But this time we were not able to go far because we met a road block. This was terrible, as the armed men who were guarding it decided they would not let us pass. We spent the whole night there and in the morning God sent a heavy rain that no one could resist. The guards had to leave and we took that opportunity to slip by without anyone interfering. That day it rained for almost 6 hours and we enjoyed the fastest travel since we had begun the journey.

At around 3 p.m. the rain finally stopped and we decided to look for a place to spend the night and rest. Road blocks were back up again. We asked someone whether there was a church nearby. He said he would take us there. He boarded one of the vehicles and went ahead of us. We thought he was so kind, since such helpful people were rare at that time. Only later did we realize that he was actually going to alert the next road block that we were suspect and therefore they shouldn't let us go through without a proper check. When we arrived at the road block, all of a sudden we were surrounded by armed men forcing everyone to get out of the cars and doing a thorough search of everything we were carrying. When I got out of the vehicle, I was unable to stand and my legs were so heavy and swollen that I was not even able to put on my slippers. Another woman told me to lie down. There was a coffee plantation right there and she put a sheet on the ground for me and I slept. The men continued with their inspection but later agreed to take us to the Anglican church, which was just few metres away saying they would check on us again later.

As for me it was going to be a long night, a night of great horror and pain, but a night where God was about to glorify Himself as He directed our firstborn's entrance into the world.

OUR FIRST MIRACLE BABY WAS BORN

Great is your faithfulness oh God my father.
There is no shadow of turning with thee;
Thou changest not, Thy compassions, they fail not
As Thou has been Thou forever will be.[‡]

Whenever I begin telling this story, I am almost speechless, as I cannot find the proper terms to describe God's greatness, faithfulness, love and compassion to me. In fact, I came to appreciate God even more when I later understood how dangerous it had been and how the baby's life was at risk. I am glad I was somewhat ignorant at that time, because if I knew then what I know now, I would have been even more afraid. In addition, I am glad for the few people who were there and sensed the danger but did not chose to reveal it to me. May God bless them all, since I never saw them after that but wherever they are, I am praying for God's favour upon their lives.

It was April 25 and I was so tired and worried. When we arrived at the church, many other people were also trying to find a place to sleep. Many went into the building, but I couldn't because I didn't feel well and needed fresh air. One woman there became like my mother and my nurse. Her name was Jane. She had known me since I was a baby, because she had been a very close friend of my mother's.

Jane had had 10 children but since she lived close to the hospital in Gahini all had been born there. At that moment, however, God gave her the knowledge she needed to support me in my desperate situation. She was the first person I approached and told how I was feeling. She immediately prayed with me and assured me that God was in total control. Jane was concerned about me and went to the pastor's house to ask for some water. Then she took me behind one of the buildings and helped me to wash. As I did so, we realized I was bleeding. She called a few other women and I could see that they were worried and confused. Jane continued praying. She gave me her shoulder to lay my head on but standing became a problem. The pain in my abdomen was increasing but would come and go. She took a watch and noted that the pain was coming every five minutes which meant I was in labour. "Now you have to be strong", she said. "Take it easy, we are going to pray and all is going to be well", she added.

I did not really believe her. She suggested that instead of going to sleep, I should walk around to hasten the labour. I agreed. I had no choice. I did not know what else to do but my legs became so weak. I was shaking. It felt like my bladder was going to burst. The bleeding did not stop. My fear and anxiety were unbearable. I asked her to let me lay down but she sat just beside me, gently massaging my back. Whenever I wanted to shout because of pain, she told me to be quiet. She said, "When you shout you are stopping your baby from getting the oxygen needed and it weakens you even more. You need enough strength to be able to push your baby out." I obeyed but it was hard.

We asked whether there were a medical centre around. We were told that there used to be one, but it was not functioning anymore. We learnt that there was a Catholic brother nearby who was a clinical officer so my husband looked for him to ask for advice. The brother did not have anything at all to help us, but he said that normally when a pregnant woman was brought to them bleeding, they had to administer some vitamin K to stop the bleeding. By God's grace, vitamin K was the one medicine we had! I took several tablets and the bleeding stopped (though later when I talked to a gynaecologist she told me that Vitamin K tablets would not stop the bleeding but rather an injection would be needed). My own conviction is when God wants to bring glory to Himself, He does things that even science can not explain. He is never limited by our knowledge and discovery; after all He is the one who controls our knowledge.

After the bleeding stopped, another frightening thing happened. A dark, thick, green liquid began to flow out of me. Again, everyone around me looked scared and confused. I could hear them asking one another, "Now what is this?" Whether they knew how to interpret what they saw I do not know. But it was clear that something was abnormal, though they did not want to tell me. Later I learned that was a sign that the baby was distressed and in great danger.

My pain was increasing. Everybody went to sleep except Jane and three other women including a 15 or 16 year old who had just joined a nursing school. She was the only expert I had around, but I have no doubt that Jesus Himself was present. They really stood with me. I later found out that Jane had had spinal cancer for many years and amazingly she is still alive and strong even today. God used her mightily to encourage me in my hour of desperate need. We were together the whole night moving around. I was so tired that sometimes I found myself asleep during labour until the pain would wake me. Jane was holding me all the time and after some hours, we could not walk anymore. We went back to the house. My husband was scared to even approach me.

A plastic sheet that we had bought on the way was laid on the ground for me. I just lay down. I was desperate. Jane looked at me and asked, "Do you still believe in miracles?" "Yes", I replied, although I was not so sure I really meant it.

Then she said, "As I was praying I saw angels from heaven coming down, and they are the ones going to help you deliver your baby, do you believe that?" I told her I wasn't sure, but she told me, "Soon you will have your baby."

Jane instructed me, "When you feel like you want to release yourself, go ahead; don't worry." She watched me, telling me what to do and what not to do.

She said, "Make sure you breathe in enough air because your baby needs it now." I tried but it was difficult. It reached a point where I was completely exhausted and felt like I wanted to release myself so she shouted, "Go ahead, do it."

I gathered all my strength and pushed down and suddenly the baby found her way out. She did not cry immediately but took about five minutes. On April 26, 1994 at 9 a.m. a slim, long, green-coloured body and head was born. The baby – a girl -- was so tired. Her skin looked wrinkled like an old woman's. She had no flesh on her bones. She looked sickly and was a strange colour. It was my first born. How did this happen? Jesus' words as uttered by Paul give a perfect answer. He says,

> 'My grace is sufficient for you, for my power is made
> perfect in weakness.' 2 Corinthians 12:9

And for sure there is no other explanation. Only by His grace did my baby and I survive. People began to sing and my husband, who had followed the progress from a distance came back singing, "Halleluiah!"

Jane asked me, "What is the first thing you want to tell God now?"

I said, "What else apart from thanking Him?"

Then with a strong voice and almost slapping me she said, "Ask for forgiveness because you doubted His power."

I agreed and felt so foolish. Thank God because He knows all our weaknesses and is always ready to forgive.

After the baby was born, the placenta came out but they were not able to check whether it was complete. The baby had torn me badly. The wound was big, but I did not care and was not thinking about infections. Again, Jane gave me some advice. She had us boil water and let it cool until it would not burn the skin but was still hot, then added salt and I sat in it. I did this three times a day and every time I could I applied some special butter (the oil locally extracted from cow's milk which was sent to me by my mother a few days before the war began). It's amazing how God prepares for us everything beforehand without our knowledge. That assured me of God's love and mercy upon my life and that of my baby. Traditionally it was believed that this oil had medicinal properties especially for keeping wounds from getting infected. I am not sure whether this is scientifically proven but at least it kept the skin soft enough to avoid cracking. I used the same oil on my baby's skin. Initially I did not like the smell, but I have learned there are times when it is no longer a matter of liking or disliking, it is a matter of survival. This way you learn to appreciate everything you have.

And God uses all manner of things like when Jesus healed the blind man. What did He use in Mark 8:23? He spat and touched the man's eye and his sight was restored. I felt Jesus' touch through many people and many insignificant things to perform extraordinary events. What doctor would prescribe children's medicine for a twenty nine year old patient? Under ordinary circumstances, no one. But here I was using some left over Septrim (sulpha antibiotic) syrup that had been prescribed for a two months old baby. When the mother brought it to me she said, "I know you need some antibiotics to take care of possible infections, and this is what I have -- maybe it will help." I took it by faith and God used it. The same morning another lady brought me some millet flour to make into porridge. That was my first food after two days without eating.

In less than two hours my baby began vomiting the thick, green fluid that she had swallowed in the delivery process. I was scared and I ran to call Jane who had now become like my mother. She came and told me, "It is good that she is able to expel these things since she is not in a hospital where this would have been taken care of differently. Just keep her in a safe position to avoid choking."

My newborn baby vomited for more that ten minutes. After that, she slept again. When she woke up, she was hungry and wanted to breastfeed. Exhausted and dehydrated, I had no milk at all. The pastor at the church learnt that a woman staying at his church had given birth but had no milk. He brought a bottle of cow's milk and I had no choice but to give it to her.

Some time later I told my birth story to Dr. Angela, a gynaecologist, and as I went on I saw the expression change on her face. So I smiled and told her, "Don't worry, my baby is alive and well". She couldn't believe it. She explained to me that the green fluid is called meconium. The meconium has three grades according to its colour and thickness which indicates how distressed a baby is. The worst grade is when it is thick and green. This is a bad sign and the baby can die or have brain damage. The brain damage is normally manifested by abnormal development and low IQ. Thank God my baby survived and thrived in spite of all that.

As we were getting ready to leave the place where I had the baby, the people who had carried us in their car said they had no more room for me since I had a baby. It sounded strange to me. Then the bishop said, "You can leave anybody else but take this woman with her baby." I thanked God for that and I urged my husband to please not give in because it was a matter of death or life. With or without the agreement of those who thought the pick up was theirs, we needed to get in since it belonged to the school where they worked and where we worked before we were transferred. The woman was almost mad at him but I told him to just keep quiet.

Three days after the baby was born, (who did not yet have a name as our tradition is to name babies on the eighth day) we resumed our journey. It was tough. I could only pray and Jane never left me. She was always with me through it all. We wanted to go to one of the other mission schools where we thought we knew people and it was a bit farther from the fighting. Getting there took us two days. God led us to a place where a medical centre had just been completed, with new buildings and nice rooms and beds. I thought at last God has given me a place to lay my head down. I was glad. The caretaker said she could only give us a place to sleep but no food. Then she said she was going to provide food only for the baby and me. She cooked very nice food and tea saying, "You must eat because your baby needs milk." That night, four days after her birth, my baby had breast milk for the first time. You can imagine how glad I was. On April 31, we made our way to a nearby school where we spent another month before proceeding.

A TIME OF RESTING

"This is the resting place, let the weary rest, and this the place of repose." Isaiah 28:12

Many people that we knew were already at the school where we rested for a month. One lady named Asinath was a nurse and took me to the house she and her family had been given to live in. She gave me some warm water to take a bath, and made some porridge and food for me. She forced me to eat it all and it was a lot! She insisted that the baby needed milk and I needed strength. She cleaned the baby. Since she was born, I had been afraid to wash her, so the whole of her body was still covered with the dry meconium. Asinath, a nurse and a pastor's wife, taught me how to clean the baby's nose and ears. I was so grateful. She didn't even know me but was offering me these kindnesses! She took me to her bed and I slept. I had not slept in such a comfortable bed for a month.

In the evening, my husband and I were given a small room to sleep in. The room was very cold and wet and the baby immediately caught the flu and a rash all over her skin. The next day we begged the people in charge of the student dormitory to let us sleep there, since the students were gone for holiday. We were given a room with a bunk bed and two small mattresses. While it was warmer than the other room, the beds were not comfortable and hurt my back so I preferred sleeping on the floor. The baby woke up several times at night and every time she woke I thought she was hungry so I fed her and sometimes she would throw up the excess milk.

Because of her rash some people told me not to put too many clothes on the baby in order to reduce sweating. Others said it was very important to dress her in several warm clothes at night so that she would not get a cold. I had so many advisors that at the end of the day I did not know the right thing to do.

The baby's flu did not clear up until I was advised to give her some amoxicillin syrup. She also had very serious constipation and I did not know what to do for that. I continued struggling with milk and it seemed I never had enough so we had to introduce some formula, which really troubled her a lot, and part of the problem was that I really did not know how to prepare it properly. Still God was so faithful and kept my baby alive despite the struggles.

On the eighth day after birth, it was time to name the baby. We made some tea and invited a few people to come and participate in the naming ceremony, according to our customs. Some people suggested names related to the situation of the moment – such as Nyanzira, meaning the one born on the road and Nyirantambara, meaning born during the war and who therefore is believed to be stubborn or the one who brings trouble. We said we wanted to give our child a name which would remind us of God's faithfulness and our gratefulness to Him. So we named her Manushimwe, a Rwandan name meaning "God be praised". On a daily basis we call her Sandrine. We do not use the Rwandan name much because she grew up outside Rwanda and not many people are able to pronounce it. Sandrine is easier for non-Rwandan speakers.

At the end of May 1994, we again had to leave, as it was obvious that the fighting was getting closer. We could hear the thunder of heavy arms in the distance. We did not know how or where to go next. The people who up to then had been carrying us had already gone away without our knowledge. We had access to a pick up that had been bought for our school. It was given to us, but my husband and I had not yet learned how to drive. God brought a young man who also was looking for a means of evacuating. Since he was a driver, our prayer was partly answered. The next challenge was to where to get petrol. Then another man appeared whose wife had had a baby. He said he had no means to travel, so he asked whether he could contribute to the petrol in order for us to go together. That suggestion was welcomed so we took off. Immediately after we left, the noise of firearms became louder and a huge crowd fleeing for their lives emerged in the town.

THE DIVIDED ROAD

"Even though I walk through the valley of the shadow of death, I will fear no evil, for you are with me."
Psalm 23:4

Until then, we had continued together with Jane, her family and some of our friends from our church. It gave us a greater sense of security when we could be with people we knew and who knew us. Now, however, when it was time to relocate, we each took a different road since none of us knew which way would be safer. It was a matter of life or death and became a personal decision as there was too much that was unknown. In a country with no proper communication, where rumours were rampant, no one could make a decision for the other. So we prayed for one another and trusted God for our safety. Most people from our group headed towards the southern part of the country but we went north.

A factor that contributed to our decision was that the person who was driving us wanted to rejoin his family. We went along and trusted God for the best. Because we were in an area where no one knew us to be able to vouch for our identity and background, our safety was tenuous. Every time we managed to be cleared at a road block we gave thanks to the Lord. At every road block there were at least 50 militia men. Their main job was to check every traveller. You needed to provide your identity card which they might or might not actually read. Many of them did not even know how to read.

When it was almost dark, we again started looking for a place to spend the night. We hoped to get into another school led by Catholic sisters, but we did not manage to reach it before nightfall. It was also hard to be received by someone who did not know you as they wanted to avoid trouble for themselves. When we stopped at one place looking for something to eat or drink the people there were suspicious of us because we were strangers in that area. One man said he would help us get some food. He boarded our pick up and went with us but when we reached the road block, he told his people a different story. They surrounded our car and we were ordered to show our IDs and get out. We were very worried because I did not have my ID.

They asked whether there was any other person in the area that knew us. My husband managed to remember that a man from his area was working in a tea factory just a few meters from where we were. He was sent for and when he came he greeted all of us in a very familiar way, calling my husband by name, asking about news from home, and so on. This man was led by the Spirit and that again demonstrated God's protection in our times of need. Still the militias did not seem totally satisfied but at last we were given permission to continue. The one who looked like their leader offered to give us shelter since it was evening. We thought that was a kind gesture, so innocently we accepted the offer and followed him.

Around 6 p.m. someone came and told us that if we were to sleep in this house we would be killed. He took us to another man's place where he had built rooms for day scholar students from two nearby secondary schools.

When the militia leader returned in the evening to the house where he had left us and found that we were gone he was furious, so he led a group of militia to follow us to the new place. At around 8 p.m. we were abruptly awakened and ordered to come out of the house. We thought this would be the end of us.

Suddenly a military officer appeared out of the blue demanding to know what was going on. The owner of the house explained the situation and the military officer dismissed the militia telling them that if there were a problem, they should come during the day, not at night. Then we were told to report to the chancellor of the area the next morning to get permission to stay. Finally we managed to sleep that night.

Our clearance was achieved the next day with the help of the owner of the rooms who was anxious to earn some cash through the rental. He even insisted that we pay three months' rent up front. We did not have enough funds but the person who was helping us with the petrol lent us enough to pay the rent. We stayed there for another month without further harassment from the militia. We were reminded of what the Lord told the prophet Isaiah and we made these words our own:

> *When you pass through the waters, I will be with you*
> *and when you pass through the rivers they will not*
> *sweep over you, when you walk through the fire you*
> *will not be burned, the flames will not set you ablaze.*
> Isaiah 43:2

POSTNATAL
COMPLICATIONS

God's unseen presence comforts me
I know He's always near.
And when life's storms besiege our soul,
He says, 'My child, I'm here'[5]

Given the circumstances of our constant movement, I was never able to have a medical check up after I gave birth. And I never had a proper time of rest either. My body continued to be weak but I did not have a good explanation for the way I felt. I also wanted to prove to the people around me that I was not a lazy woman and that I could take good care of my baby and husband as was culturally expected. So even when I needed help, I rarely asked. Everyone was preoccupied with their own situation and didn't really notice how I was doing. Over time though, my health continued to deteriorate.

When Sandrine was nearly six weeks old, I developed a very bad fever. I thought it was malaria so I bought some anti-malaria tablets and painkillers, but the fever did not go down. On top of that, the bleeding had never totally stopped since I had given birth.

I just thought it was because I had never rested sufficiently. Finally I visited a health centre which had also been badly affected by the war and had next to no supplies. The sisters who ran it had fled the country. The health workers still there only injected me every time I went for a visit to try to control the bleeding but they were unable to bring it under control and the fever was still high.

During this time Deo was able to obtain a travel document for me from the district immigration department which was located in a town some 10 km from where we were living and less than a kilometre from the Congolese border. With that in hand he was able to take me to the only hospital which was still functioning in the whole country. By God's grace, we found a gynaecologist there. As I told him my story I could read his mind from his face – he was gravely concerned. He asked me to get on the examining table. After his examination, he announced that some of the placenta had remained in my womb and had become very infected. He insisted that he had to remove the parts of the placenta which were causing infection in the uterus, and for that, he needed to put me to sleep under general anaesthesia.

I refused insisting that, "There is no way you could make me sleep! I had left my baby and there was a war raging around us. I needed to be alert and active to care for my family and stay on the move." Seeing my conviction, he asked whether I was ready to let him do the curettage without anaesthesia, because my life was in danger if I wasn't treated immediately. I agreed.

Today I cannot recall what that operation was like. I don't know whether I fainted from the pain, or whether God supernaturally shielded me from it, but I remember no pain. When the operation was finished, the doctor showed me what he had removed. He was surprised; he said very few women would have the courage to go through such an operation unmedicated. I was given some antibiotics and was booked for another appointment. The wound healed and the bleeding stopped within a few days. I never made it for the next appointment because that day everyone had to leave the town. When I talked to another gynaecologist to understand all the medical and health implications of my situation, she explained to me that normally when the placenta is not completely removed from the uterus the mother dies within a matter of days or even hours. Additionally, when these infections occur in the uterus, it is almost impossible to have another baby. By the grace of God none of these unfortunate things happened to me and I later had five more children! Our God is not limited by science or medical probabilities or our logic. He is the one who created our minds, He controls them and our minds are too small to accommodate God's mind and therefore we are unable to comprehend everything He does. He says, *"I am the Lord who heals you."* Exodus 15:26

THE JOURNEY INTO THE JUNGLE

"You need not fear where you are going when God is going with you."[6]

For the next three days I was on medication, but before it was finished, I began to feel uncomfortable and apprehensive about some danger. The houses we were living in were surrounded by very dense banana plantations. You could not see even 300 meters away. We could see huge crowds flowing again day in and day out which had become a sign of heavy fighting taking place in the area. Rumours were circulating that Kigali, the capital city had already been conquered by the RPF. I sensed that the time to move on was at hand. I had heard testimonies of women who lost their babies, either because they were caught up by surprise by guns shooting outside their homes and were not able to get back to their families, or because they simply got confused and somehow were separated from their children. I thought that was the worst thing that could happen to me. Based on my feelings we immediately went into town.

Our initial plans were not to stay in town but to get travel documents for my sister-in-law and our house helper who were with us. We were at the border with Congo (then called Zaire), and we knew if the fighting found us there the only option left was to cross over to Congo but we were scared to go beyond the frontier of Rwanda.

We did not manage to get the papers we needed in one day so we had to sleep in another church compound in the city hoping to get the papers the next day. That same night, the militia invaded the compound where we had been staying. The people who remained there were robbed, but the militia were specifically looking for our pick up which was brand new. Fortunately for us, it was no longer there.

Towards dawn the following day, even the town was bombed. We had no choice but to cross the border into Congo without the papers we were seeking. I asked him to buy some medicines and formula for Sandrine. I was not worried about myself. He bought several items including Septrim (a sulpha antibiotic), anti-malaria medication, and a medicine for worms. Of course, I was only guessing when I asked him to buy these -- just trying to remember what I had seen other mothers give to their babies.

On July 14, 1994, we crossed the border from Rwanda into Congo. We had the pick up but it could not move because of the crowd. We did not want to wait for the worst. We decided that my husband and the driver would stay with the car to try to drive it slowly through the crowd. Another young man who had gone the previous day to Goma in Congo, said he had seen an Anglican Archbishop at his church who could easily give me a place to sleep with my baby as we waited for my husband to cross the border. So we decided to leave the car and go on foot to the church in Congo. I was so weak that I was not able to carry Sandrine. My sister-in-law carried her on her back and I walked just behind her to protect the baby from being suffocated by the press of people in the crowd. The distance from the Rwanda - Congo border to the church where we were headed in the town of Goma was less than two kilometres. But it took us more than three hours to walk that distance and it took my husband more than 8 hours to come with the car. At the Anglican church in Goma we were accommodated in the church building. Within a few minutes, the building was so full that we had to go outside to get some fresh air. A completely new life as foreigners and refugees had begun.

The first challenge was to find safe drinking water. Sandrine was tied on my back continuously. There was no place to put her down to sleep. My breastmilk was completely gone. She had to drink formula, but I did not have water to prepare it. The Vicar of the church took me to his house and gave some water, but it was not clean enough. Sandrine became sick the following day. She was throwing up and had severe diarrhoea which was very scary. Without consulting anyone, I gave her the Septrim syrup but it did not help her improve. Fortunately, we met a doctor. He prescribed some drops to stop the vomiting. By God's grace, the vomiting ceased and I continued with the antibiotic. Still Sandrine was very weak, with no proper feeding.

Hygiene was very poor, and there were dead bodies all over the place. Many people died of cholera and dysentery, others died of dehydration and fatigue. You might be sitting near someone and all of a sudden you would realize that they were dead and that you are in the midst of corpses. I can not forget a woman who died when seated right next to me. She had just arrived and was breathing very fast like someone who had been racing. She sat down and someone offered some rice they had just cooked. She started eating but suddenly died with the rice still in her mouth. I was so traumatized and up to now that picture has not left my mind. Within a very short time the whole town was full of corpses because there was no place to bury them. The bodies started decomposing which brought clouds of flies. Everything was contaminated. Mobile radio stations started educating people about not eating fruits or any other uncooked foods. The water was also contaminated and the air pollution was unimaginable. All of us wondered whether we were still alive or dead. Looking at these circumstances there was little hope that we would survive.

Fortunately, Pat, a British missionary who happened to be in the town of Goma at that time, was moved by the misery of the people around her. She was the first person to provide help in terms of food and blankets. She also hired a lorry to bring water to us. I am saddened by the fact that she will not see my book. She is in heaven now and my prayer is that I may see her on that last day. I also remember the vicar of the church, who is now the Anglican bishop of Kindu diocese in DRC, The Right Reverend Masimango Katanda, telling me, "Even if other people miss food I will make sure you are served so that you can feed your baby." This servant of God had also allowed us to sleep in his own office at the church.

He said, "There is no way that baby can sleep outside and since I do not have room in my house, just use my office and in the morning you can take your things out so that we can continue our work." That was so kind and we really saw the love of God manifested to us through Bishop Masimango. May God continue to bless him abundantly, and may He expand his territory.

At one point during this period, I was unable to stand anymore. My back and my legs were very weak and shaking. The bleeding had returned and for three days we had no water to even wipe our face or rinse our mouths.

There were few places for people to relieve themselves, and those that were available were terrible. However, after three days it was impossible for me to hold myself. I had to try a public latrine. This was just a hole and few pieces of wood on top of it. At first, I was scared but finally decided to hold my breath and go in. As I was trying to place my foot on one of the pieces of wood, I slipped and was left hanging between two pieces of wood. I screamed. Fortunately, there were people around who immediately came and pulled me out. They looked for some water and tried to clean the mess from my body. However, as you can imagine, I was definitely not very clean, so I didn't want to hold my baby.

That evening, I went to Pastor Masimango's house and was given some water to wash off. I went and hid behind their small house to take a bath. After I had taken off all my clothes a bomb was thrown at the international airport of Goma, not very far from where we were. Without remembering where I was and what I was doing, I just ran, still naked. Thank God it was night time. After a few minutes, I went back, bathed very quickly and was able to feel a bit of freshness again.

The number of dead continued to increase and bodies were everywhere in Goma. Following the bombing at the airport, thousands of people perished. That is when the first organization was sent to Goma to help clean the city by burying the dead. One of our friends' children had the same sickness as Sandrine and died. Seeing the parents wait for the lorry carrying the dead in order to place their child's body on it to be buried with the others was so depressing. I prayed even more fervently that God would provide special protection for my baby.

One Sunday morning the pastor announced at church that in

his office there was a child who was sick (Sandrine). Immediately after the service, a lady came into our room. She introduced herself as a Rwandan who had lived in Congo for many years and she asked if she could pray for my baby. I said, "Sure, you are welcome to do so." She came and prayed and I trusted God for her healing.

In the evening of the same day, a pastor from a neighbouring Lutheran church came to visit our refugee camp. He said he had a room for a pastor with a small family. Immediately people thought of us and when we were told, we took it as an answer from God. We immediately went and were put in one of the church offices, which was much better than where we were staying before. There was plenty of water at this Lutheran church compound and immediately we took a proper bath. Then we washed our clothes and we had some rice, powdered milk, and beans. It was our first meal in almost a week.

Our five months at the Lutheran Church were such a blessing. Signs of life began to be evident again. Electricity and water were supplied free of charge. Sandrine was introduced to solid foods as formula became too expensive. The World Lutheran Church sent food (rice, beans), blankets, plastic sheets, medications and a doctor along with some money to buy shoes for the people who were at the Lutheran church in Goma. My condition had not improved, so as soon as the doctor came I was the first person to be seen. He gave me some strong antibiotics and watched me closely. What a blessing!

Somehow, in the midst of all this sickness, upheaval, and

discomfort, when Sandrine was six months old, I conceived our second baby but I did not know I was pregnant until I found myself not wanting to eat food again.

LIFE IN THE REFUGEE CAMP

*"Christ's presence is clearly our provision for all we
need, our hidden manna for surviving life's journey"[7]*

In August 1994, a humanitarian agency called Church World Action (CWA) came looking for people from different denominations to work in a refugee camp. My husband was recruited as one of the staff. He was not sure whether he should accept the offer but I encouraged him. His supervisor was a pastor from the Netherlands named Henry, who became a very good friend and God used him to bless us in many ways. The camp in which my husband worked was not where we lived. Every day he had to make a round trip of about 30 km. to get there.

At the end of December 1994, two months after my husband began working at the refugee camp, the insecurity became so severe in Goma that we had to move to the camp. The Congolese soldiers were harassing people, asking for money or taking goods by force. They would even follow you to the market and after you bought food they would demand that you give them everything you bought. They also wanted to take the pick up. A number of times they confiscated it and would ask us to pay a lot of money to get it back. The last time was what caused us to choose to go to the camp; they forced the person who was driving the truck out and drove it to what they called their offices. When we went for it, they said that if we did not give them $2000, even my husband was going to be put in prison. At his place of work they immediately held a meeting to discuss the matter, the organization agreed to pay for him, and we got the car back. We knew that the next time things would be even worse.

We had a tent that we had been able to buy for $70 immediately after crossing the border into Congo when we had been able to make some money by selling firewood. Our small pickup was used to carry people from Goma to the camp area and on the way back they would bring firewood to sell.

That tent became our house for the next three months in the camp but the cold was hard to bear, especially for Sandrine. She developed chronic respiratory illness and infections which often turned into pneumonia. She also had severe eczema and diarrhoea became her way of life. She grew very thin. I thought the porridge I was feeding her was too soft so I stopped sifting it which made her situation even worse. As her skin became even rougher, in my ignorance I kept changing soaps (mostly antiseptic) hoping they would help. Nothing I tried did any good. Sometimes I did not want people to look at her.

Sandrine was completely weaned in her sixth month and became an object of learning for her inexperienced mother. I made so many and sometimes very dangerous mistakes. But our God who is so merciful, who understands our weaknesses and rectifies our mistakes, took her through that. How can I praise Him? Like the prophet Isaiah, I will forever say,

"O Lord, you are my God;

I will exalt you and praise your name,

For in perfect faithfulness you have done marvellous things,

things planned long ago." Isaiah 25:1

As a young and inexperienced mother, Sandrine's many sicknesses were hard on me as well. She was always on antibiotics. Most of the time I carried her on my back, even at night when she was unable to sleep. I was very tired from lack of sleep and from my pregnancy.

I made so many mistakes when it came to feeding her and treating her skin. Many times I laid her down and let her feed herself. I prepared her bottle, placed it on a pillow and inserted the nipple into her mouth so I could continue with my work. Little did I know that it was very easy for her to choke. One day I found her struggling. She had finished the bottle and fell asleep on her back when she spit up some of the milk she had just drunk. Because of her position, the milk went back into her mouth and nose. I was so scared and never did it again. That was one of the many lessons that I had to learn.

One morning and after a long, tiring night, I asked a young girl who was living with us to carry Sandrine for me so that I could have a bit of rest. I went to sleep but before long, I heard Sandrine screaming. When I ran out I saw that Sandrine was in agony, her arm red and raw, terribly burned. At that time she did not yet know how to sit properly and the girl had set her next to a charcoal cooker which had some hot water on it. Sandrine had fallen into the cooker, spilling the hot water onto her arm as she fell. The way she had fallen, it would have been possible for her to have burned her whole body, but God spared her life.

That experience was a nightmare. I rushed to the clinic, accompanied by a neighbour but they could not do much for my baby. For the next two days, I spent my nights outside the house; Sandrine's fever was too high and keeping her inside the plastic sheet house only made things worse. The plastic sheet houses would get too hot on sunny days and cold at night. But also they were so small that when you had many people sleeping in one house, even the oxygen was not enough, making it even more uncomfortable. For a child struggling with fresh burn wounds it was tough. I was thoroughly exhausted as I spent this time carrying two babies day and night, one in the womb and the other on my back. Sandrine cried incessantly in excruciating pain that I could not relieve. She would not accept anyone else except me, as most young children do when they are in pain. They think their mothers have all the answers even when they don't. I thank God for His strength to endure that time, and His protection on Sandrine's life. That was the most painful experience I had in the refugee camp. Added to the physical pain was the fact that I received no word of encouragement from anyone. My husband was also confused not knowing what to do. Since he worked far from where we lived, he usually left home very early and came back late in the evening. I had to do most of the work for Sandrine. Neighbours would accuse me of being a careless mother. I felt so inadequate, so incapable and at same time I tried to hide behind my mask. I had gotten myself a job as a social worker to try to satisfy my desire to be a valuable woman. In my work I was a pastor's wife who was supposed to be a super woman, all knowing, and a counsellor for others. I had to look like I was different from the rest. Many times I was able to counsel other women only by the grace and favour of God.

Today Sandrine still carries a scar from the burn on her arm and every time I see it, I give thanks to the Lord, because I could have lost her completely.

During those months in the refugee camp in Congo, we had no news from our parents and siblings. Sometimes when the pressure was too great, I would hide and cry. Many times, I felt abandoned under the burden I had to carry. I wondered why all this was happening to me. Nevertheless, every time my spirit was low, my thoughts were taken back to memories of the recent past. I constantly thought of Sandrine's miraculous birth. I remembered that many of our friends and relatives had perished because of the war, so the fact that we were still alive and united as a family gave me reason to smile despite the challenges.

In the refugee camp there were a number of organisations providing various services including medical care. Now that I was again expecting, my prayer was that I would have a proper place to deliver my baby. To my surprise, when I went to the clinic for the first time, I met the gynaecologist who had done the curettage just before we crossed over to Congo. He recognized me and since he knew important parts of my history, he was able to provide proper treatment and advice. What a relief! I attended the clinic regularly. The hospital facilities were just a tent with some beds and mattresses. It had a few qualified nurses and at least two medical doctors. They were able to handle normal deliveries, but if there were any complications which required an operation, the hospital was inadequate. I prayed for a normal delivery.

The baby did not come by the due date and after waiting two more weeks, I was to be induced; I was given some fluid to drink to bring on labour. I spent the night of August 1, 1995, in the refugee camp "hospital". This time things were so peaceful.

There was no bombing, nurses were there to monitor labour and delivery and there was a bed for me to sleep on. We had some lanterns for lighting the tent. When labour began there was no bleeding but a gush of meconium preceded the baby. I could read panic on the nurses' faces. However, since I had seen that and worse during my first delivery, it did not bother me too much. After all, no one had yet explained to me the implications of having such a discharge before the baby was born.

The nurses watched me the whole night and at 5 a.m. on August 2, 1995, my second child was born. I was singing on the delivery table, "Halleluiah! Praise the Lord!" In the morning when Deo came, I was sleeping with our baby. He was amazed and didn't want to disturb me so he left for work as usual. I spent the whole day in the hospital without much food. In the evening I was very hungry and could not feed the baby. When he came back he took me home.

After eight days, we had the naming ceremony for our second child. It was also a time to celebrate the life of our first daughter and God's love and mercy. Both our children were living testimonies of God's faithfulness and we wanted always to be reminded of that. We therefore called our second daughter, "Christine Haleluya," in other words, let Christ in us be praised for who He has been and will continue to be forever and ever.

Two weeks after Christine was born, insecurity became too high in the camp. Congolese soldiers had invaded and were beating people and looting property such as mattresses, radios, cars and money, and some of the refugees had become desperate because of the harsh camp life. Support had declined and there was no longer enough food. So the refugees themselves had begun targeting those who had any kind of income. It was scary to stay in our tent. For two days, we had to hide in the bush with our babies. My husband's supervisor told him that he needed to buy a tent and wondered whether he could buy ours. He said that normally a new tent like that would cost $2000 but that he could give us $1500. We thought that was a dream since we had paid only $70 for it. We agreed but thought he might change his mind. In fact, he paid us what he offered which was definitely another miracle and we no longer needed the tent because the camp had become insecure and we needed to leave.

At that time, my husband had planned to visit Nairobi to see if it might be possible for me to settle there as he continued with his work to support us as a family. The day he was supposed to travel no movement was allowed from the camps to the town as the situation had become life threatening. In fact, I was glad that he did not travel at that time.

On the third day of hiding in the bush, one of my husband's colleagues took the risk to come and evacuate us from the camp to Goma town. We thank God for him. We were given shelter in a small tent as we waited for the situation to calm down. I was determined that I was not going to go back to the refugee camp. I needed a more secure place for my babies and to rest.

Pastor Masimango helped us get air tickets and on August 30, 1995 when Christine was four weeks old, we flew to Nairobi. She was very tiny but beautiful - definitely another miracle baby.

Below are the comments from Dr Angela, a gynaecologist in Nairobi, after she listened to my story:

> *Sandrine and Christine seemed to have suffered lack of oxygen while in the womb, a condition known as foetal distress. Considering the period of time they stayed within the womb under such conditions one would have expected them to have a degree of brain damage evidenced by delayed development, delayed milestones and lower IQ (intelligence quotient). Some children even develop some palsy or weakness. It can only be a miracle that their growth and development has been normal. You suffered both ante partum (before birth) and post partum (after birth) haemorrhage (bleeding), which greatly weakens a woman and increases the risk of dying. Retention of a part of the placenta in the uterus for so long resulting in infection, in most cases affects the woman's ability to have babies later. The tubes often get blocked and the uterus scarred. In your case this did not happen, as evidenced by the five additional children you have had. It can only be God.*

Our God still performs miracles! I wonder whether you believe in Him. If you do, do not give up. If you do not, what are you waiting for?

STRANGERS IN A NEW LAND

Cursed is the man who withholds justice from the alien,
the fatherless or the widow. Deuteronomy 27:19

In August 1995, we arrived in Nairobi, Kenya. We knew of a number of people who had come before us but did not know how to reach them. At the airport, we had to fill out papers, a task I left to my husband. He had to dig into his mind to find some English vocabulary to use. Ahead of him there was a long queue and many people were refused entry visas. When his turn came to hand in the forms, he was not sure what would happen. All of a sudden we saw a pastor from our country who we knew. He had arrived some months previously and studied both in Kenya and America. He was at the airport to fetch someone else who never showed up. When he saw us, he knew we needed help and immediately came and helped with the forms, and was able to answer some of the questions we were not able to answer. We were given a visa. Behind us a friend was almost sent back but we told our pastor that we knew him and explained to the immigration officers that we were together so he also was given a visa. The pastor took us to his house where we spent a week while looking for our own place to stay.

A year in the camp had impacted our lives in many ways, and we found it very difficult to adjust to life in Nairobi. We had been used to a completely different lifestyle. In spite of the obvious hardships in camp there were some advantages to life there. Most everything had been free -- food, water, medical care and housing (since we supplied our own). In Nairobi, we had to pay for everything -- housing, food, water, medicines, and medical consultations. And the biggest challenge was language. For the first time we found ourselves in a community that spoke several languages, none of which we understood. We also had to get used to a new currency. Many times we found ourselves paying three times the price of items from the shops or market, simply because people took advantage of our ignorance. Learning to navigate the heavy traffic, the crazy public transportation system, and the high cost of living were other challenges.

Sandrine also had to adjust to life in new surroundings. When we arrived at the Jomo Kenyatta airport in Nairobi Sandrine just lay down on the floor because it felt so smooth to her. Up until then she had felt only rough floor surfaces. I had to struggle to keep her from being stepped on by the many people at the airport.

My husband had to go back to Goma and he thought that it was not wise to leave me alone in my own house with the children. So we lived with a friend's family who had come some months before us. At least they had learned some of the local culture, they knew how to get food, they could teach us how to board a transit van (*"matatu"*) while it was moving, and how to use local money. Living in a stone house was hard for Sandrine, who only had known plastic sheet houses and tents. Moving around on the floor was hard because she was so scared. The weather was cold. We had never experienced such cold weather before and we were not prepared. Both babies struggled with the cold for some time. I was afraid to go out and I felt lonely and a bit depressed. I wanted somebody to talk to, but I couldn't find anyone. The family we lived with had three children and together with mine there were five children in the house. I was given a bedroom for the three of us. The other children slept in the sitting room.

I couldn't sleep as the bed was too small for the three of us.

Sandrine who was only 18 months old wanted my attention and always wanted to sleep between me and her baby sister. In the end none of us slept well and we ended up being very stressed. Of course in the morning I was expected to help with the housework as well as taking care of my babies. There were three other families in the compound where we lived and some of them were gossiping about how lazy I was, since I was not able to mop the house. I remember one day when I did mop the house, and in the evening I was not even able to stand. My backache and bleeding were very bad. Immediately I thought of looking for my own rented house where I could do my own things without being a burden to anybody else. Fortunately God was gracious and I was able to locate another house where I wanted to move and after buying some of the utensils I needed, my husband returned after being gone for a month.

In November, 1995, we were finally able to move into our own rented flat. It was on the second floor and there was no water in the building so it had to be carried in from outside. I constantly had a backache and was not able to see a doctor because it was too expensive. Somehow I knew I needed rest but I was not able to get it.

Taking care of my two babies was my main occupation. I was wondering why we had to be in Kenya, a country where life seemed impossible to me.

"Wasn't it possible to study in a French speaking country where I could also find something to do?" I kept wondering. My husband insisted that he wanted to learn English and Kenya was the place to learn it. It made me nervous, but what do you do when you have to submit?

My husband immediately began his English classes at the Language Centre. I also wanted to learn but it was too expensive for both of us to study. Staying at home was depressing so I signed up for a computer class, which I only attended for a week before I stopped because of language barriers. It was impossible to communicate with my teacher and I realized it was a waste of time and money. Later we learned there was a Rwandan lady who was teaching computer so I enrolled in that course. She taught in French which made it much easier. I also enjoyed getting out of the routine of looking after babies, cooking and washing nappies. But the course only lasted two months. Together with having English classes, my husband moved around searching for a school because we did not want to spend our lives begging and feeling sorry for ourselves. I did not have a lot of faith, but I told myself we'd wait and see. Soon though, God blessed my husband's efforts for His own glory. Many people were watching him, scornful and mocking, and we finally decided we were going to NEGST (the Nairobi Evangelical Graduate School of Theology) which came as a surprise to many. As the writer of Proverbs said,

A man's heart plans his way, but the Lord directs his steps. Proverbs 16:9

And also I take these words to be true of our lives as a family: *The worst criticism of you can bring out the best in you.*[8]

We learned not to care about what other people say or think about us, we only have to learn to hear what God has for us in each moment of our lives. We have seen Him continually take us very carefully from one level to the next.

NAIROBI EVANGELICAL GRADUATE SCHOOL OF THEOLOGY (NEGST)

A HOME AWAY FROM HOME

I was hungry and you gave me something to eat, I was thirsty and you gave me something to drink, I was a stranger and you invited me in. Matthew 25:35

Going to NEGST was another incredible miracle from God. The application process had begun way back while we were still in Congo but with little progress. Communication was a huge issue. When we were finally able to come to Nairobi, the first thing we did was to visit NEGST. It located in the Karen area, in the extreme west sector of Nairobi city. We were accepted immediately when my husband presented his English certificate. The problem now was how to get the money. Meanwhile, he had also received an admission letter from the Nazarene University.

When we looked at the fee structures from both NEGST and Nazarene University, the latter was much less expensive but they did not have student housing. That meant we would have to look for a new house to rent close to the University. Before we made the final decision we met Pastor Felicien and his wife Suzan at a friend's wedding. We did not know each other but when they learnt we were from Rwanda they approached us. This was not common because many times when people learnt you were coming from the camps they kept their distance. They knew you had no money so they were afraid you might bother them with your problems. God used this family who is so dear to us to this day in mighty ways. As we were sharing, we mentioned our future plans and said we were considering joining Nazarene University since NEGST seemed too expensive.

Pastor Felicien and his wife Suzan, had just graduated from NEGST. They strongly encouraged us to go to NEGST and told us about the possibility of getting a scholarship once we were enrolled. They went on describing life at the school and said so many good things about the college that we were convinced and never regretted our decision. We were particularly touched by the way God used this couple at that particular time without them even knowing us, while people we thought would help us were strongly discouraging us by telling us how impossible it would be for us to make it financially and academically in NEGST. Thank God for good friends who are brought our way exactly when we need them!

From our savings we were able to pay our deposit, which was at that time $2000. After payment was made, we were given a nice flat, fully furnished, with a cooker, a fridge, enough beds for all of us, and plenty of running water. It was unbelievable. For two years we had not slept on a bed.

Mrs. Wood was the chairperson of the scholarship committee. She gave us addresses to write to and God used many people from all over the world to support us for four years. When I think about it I have no words. I am just amazed at how far God can take you.

Life at the Graduate School of Theology was a whole new experience. NEGST was not like schools I had known before. More than just a school, it was a family. For the first time in two years, I was able to experience a loving community. It was a multilingual, multiracial, multicultural community and such a home away from home for many of us. At first it was not easy to interact with people from all those various backgrounds. The exposure was good but frightening at the same time. We met a number of other Rwandans who had been students there for a while. It was always comfortable to be with them, as we were able to talk in our mother tongues. It was fascinating to listen to their experiences at NEGST and bit by bit we felt relieved and at home.

The last week of August 1996, was orientation week. All the new students and their spouses had to attend. I remember the academic dean, Dr. Bowen, speaking and I could hardly understand a word of his speech. He was a huge, tall man with an authoritative look and voice and he lead our first chapel. He was evidently humorous. I saw and heard people laughing and wondered what they were laughing about. He was a good singer too. He led the first hymn in our chapel, "All Hail the Power of Jesus' Name". I thought, "I have not heard such voices before." Though I was not able to understand the words, it ministered to my heart very deeply.

The spirit of fellowship was impressive and encouraging. Watching those African (a few), Western, and Asian professors chatting with us as we drank tea outside the chapel was fantastic. Since we were new, many people come up to us and talked to us in a friendly manner. I remember Mrs. Wood, one of the professor's wives who was then in charge of student scholarships speaking to me with her American accent and a big smile. Her first question was, 'What is your first name?' I partly understood. I knew she wanted to know my name but I did not know what she meant by "first" name. A fellow Rwandan colleague who was following our conversation explained to me, so then I told her I was called Clene (pronounced Clen). She asked a number of questions and my friend translated them for me and also translated my answers for Mrs. Wood. She could read the frustration on my face but she encouraged me. She said, "We have had many women in the past who, just like you, were unable to speak English when they came, but by the time they left this college they were fluent. You also will make it." I thought that was a nice encouragement but never believed it would come true for me.

After the orientation week, classes began immediately. I did not think I would be attending any. Then a missionary couple who had lived in Rwanda for many years serving in the Free Methodist Church, Rev. Martha and Jim Kirkpatrick told me that no one at that school just sits at home without going to class. Since they spoke fluent Kinyarwanda, the national and vernacular language spoken in Rwanda, they were able to explain in a way that I could understand. They said that there was a program for everyone. Indeed, there were a number of other women from Ethiopia, Chad, Congo, Togo and Tanzania who did not know English. I was happy because I was able to speak French to those from Chad, Congo and Togo.

The class we attended was referred to as 'Special English Class'. It was designed for people who had never had English at all before. After one week we were given a test and I was moved to the next class. I was wondering how long it would take me to be fluent in English and eventually be able to go to substantive Bible classes. I was impatient. All of a sudden, my latent desire to learn was reactivated. I borrowed a series of grammar books and decided to learn by myself and at my own speed. The books were small in size, so I was able to carry them around as I carried on with my daily duties. I had a small English/French dictionary for complicated words. Alongside the grammar books, I had to read some story books for children to gain vocabulary while at the same time learning how those grammatical rules were applied.

When I took my formal grammar course, I got 100% on my exam. I remember picking up my paper from my mail box. A Nigerian lady who had taken the same exam looked at my paper and said, 'That paper is not yours, the teacher made a mistake and put in somebody else's paper.' I told her to read the name. When she was finally convinced that it was indeed my paper, she asked me, 'How did you do it? You hardly speak!' I told her, 'I don't know.' After that class, I took a composition class in which I also did very well. That was the end of our first year.

The thought of taking some courses in the Masters program was taking root. I sought the advice of the registrar, who was then Mrs. Cole from Nigeria. She encouraged me and said, "Go ahead, you can do it." She talked to the academic dean, Dr. Bowen, who did not think it was a good idea. He finally agreed to allow me to take two courses at my own risk. If I failed, that would be the end of my Masters attempt.

Mrs. Cole told me not to enrol in any specific program but to register for some general courses (interdepartmental courses) which could be transferred to any of the programs if I was to be registered as a full time student. I began as a special student, meaning I was a part-time student, taking the few courses I was allowed to take for credit. Therefore I was supposed to meet all the requirements for those two courses. It was a real adventure. Some people really discouraged me, telling me that I was going to make myself look ridiculous. The people who I thought were close to me were the ones to discourage me. But I remember telling one lady that I had nothing to lose if I went to class. After all, failing a course was nothing unusual.

Choosing courses was another issue. I gave my husband that task. He advised me to take Greek, since it did not require a lot of writing and he promised he was going to help me. He had taken it before and was very good in it. He also chose a course called 'Introduction to research methods' which was basically an introduction to library research and writing papers. Those two courses were required for all the first year students.

In September 1997, I began my first year in the masters program. I was the only woman in that class and I never spoke. The teachers thought I was not following. But actually what happened was that since we had textbooks, I always learned from the book as it was truly hard to catch everything that the teachers said in class. When I took the first quiz in Greek I finished before everyone else. Next to me was sitting a Korean student, and I wanted to borrow his ruler. The teacher thought I wanted to ask him some answers. He immediately came over, took my paper looked at it and asked me what I wanted. I told him I was just borrowing a ruler to draw some lines. He said, "You don't need to do that. Can I take your paper then?" I said, "Yes".

When he brought the papers back I had gotten everything right. I did the same in the next week's quiz. He was finally convinced that I was a good student in Greek. He used to tell the other students to come to me for explanations. Of course no one came since all of them were men.

The other course I took was taught by Dr. Bowen, an American lady, who was then the NEGST Librarian. She always wondered what I was doing in her class. In all the assignments she gave us, I never got a grade higher than a C because even if I did well she thought my husband had done the work for me. The most painful experience I had in this course was with the term paper which required us to produce a Reference list of 20 books, all of them talking about the same topic. For every book we were supposed to write one to two sentences stating the theme of the book. It was not hard for me at all and I believed I had done it well. When she read my paper, she called me in her office and asked me whether I had done that paper myself. I assured her that I had.

Next she asked how I had done it. I explained in my broken English but was not able to convince her. When she gave us our grades I had a D. I cried but I did not lose hope; after all, the exams were still coming. I had passed the mid-term exam with a B. When the final exam came, I made sure I put in extra time as I prepared it. After she marked it, Dr. Bowen called me into her office again. I was scared. This time she greeted me with a smile, and she said, 'Do you know you have the highest mark on my exam?' I was overjoyed. She immediately reported it to her husband, the academic dean, who also called me into his office. He looked at my grades in both courses I took and said, "I have no right to refuse you regular student status now. Just tell me which courses you want to take."

The following term I was allowed to take three courses. I was told to consult with my academic advisor, who was then the head of the Translation Department, Dr. Ruth Mason. She asked me whether I would like to join her department. Without knowing what to expect, I accepted and asked her to suggest courses that I would begin with. She chose Grammar and Semantics in addition to the next course in Greek. She was the one teaching Semantics and promised to provide extra help for me. I took these three classes by faith. They were the first linguistic courses I had ever had. Semantics sounded too abstract. Grammar was full of new terms and vocabulary, but it was fun since for the first time I was made to examine and discover my own mother tongue. I was impressed by the fact that the teacher, Dr. George Huttar, was able to tell me how my language functioned just by looking at the little data that I provided. I enjoyed the mentorship that I received from all my teachers, especially at that early stage.

ANOTHER UNEXPECTED GIFT

"Every good and perfect gift is from above, coming down from the Father of the heavenly lights, who does not change like shifting shadows." James 1:17

In September 1998, I was finally accepted as a full-time student. I was now used to the system and was confident. My load was reduced since I had already taken eight courses. That gave me room to find time to look for a work scholarship to pay for our living expenses. The scholarship we had from the school covered only the tuition fees. The good thing was that our children were still young, so we did not yet have their school fees to worry about. But the fact that they were young meant they needed me most of the time. There was a nursery school where they spent part of the day and I made sure I did what needed to be done before they came home. My days were very busy. My school work was done only at night after the children went to bed. My usual time to go to bed was normally any time after one o'clock in the morning. Sometimes I went to bed after four in the morning because I had to maximize the time when there was little disturbance. I was constantly tired and often discouraged.

During this period, I unexpectedly conceived a third baby. It was tough, but I took it easy. I asked God for special strength and He gave it to me. The only thing I was not able to do was to do heavy work that we normally did during the long holiday to get a little more money. I had to protect myself and my baby. I attended my classes as usual and I was given a work scholarship to do the filing in the library. It was much lighter than the work I had done before, sweeping and mopping a number of classes and offices within the University.

I had to miss the second term of that academic year because my third baby was born in the first week of the term. Just before the baby was born, I wondered where I was going to get the money to pay the hospital bill. At that time we found out that that some people had sent us money through the school. We asked whether we could have it since we were expecting a baby. We were told that the money was to be used to pay my fees. I was bitter. I could not understand why the school would do that to us in the name of following the policy. But my husband always told me to cool down that the same God who had provided for us before was going to do so even now and in the future. I did not doubt that but it did not take away the bitterness.

One day as I was doing my assignment at home, a young man who was living upstairs came with an envelope. Since he was a single man, I was joking with him, asking him whether that was a wedding invitation. He smiled as he passed the envelope to me saying, 'This is for you.' He left immediately. When I opened the envelope there was KSH 1000 (almost $15). I was humbled and when I told my husband, he said, "Do you still doubt God's provision?" I asked God to forgive me.

I began a season of prayer with one of my friends. This was my first time to have a baby in Kenya, and I had always been told that it was very expensive and most of the time women are operated on with C-sections, even when it is not necessary. I used to wake up in the middle of the night when everyone else was asleep to go and pray. One night, when I was praying, I read my Bible and God gave me Isaiah 45:2-3:

> *I will go before you and will level the mountains;*
> *I will break down gates of bronze and cut through*
> *bars of iron.*
> *I will give you the treasures of darkness, riches stored*

in secret places,
so that you may know that I am the LORD, the God
of Israel, who summons you by name.

After reading it, I had peace and I thought that God was giving promises and decided to go by those.

When the baby finally came on January 8, 1999, it was a normal delivery after induction. Another daughter!! It was a different experience altogether from the previous two births, as you can imagine. The baby was born in the hospital in Nairobi. During the pregnancy, I had had ultrasounds done for the first time. I was given a comfortable room to stay in. Many friends, including my colleagues, came to visit me in the hospital. We stayed for one day and went home. We feared that the bill would be too high if I stayed longer.

At home for the first time, I saw people coming with gifts. Everyone who came to see the baby came with a gift. This was something that I had never had before. She received clothes that she wore until she was more than a year old. For the next four months we did not have to buy food. She was the smartest baby I have ever had. She was given a baby playpen. She had a number of toys. Every morning people would come in to give me some food or help me wash the baby. Women would tell me that when you gave birth you are supposed to rest, eat and sleep.

The time came to give our new daughter her name. We looked at all that had been provided for us. We went back to what God had done for us in the past and what he was doing then. We decided to call our third baby "Aviel", meaning God is my Father.

Surely, He had treated us as favoured children. And our prayer was that He would always appear to us as a father. Looking at our God as our finality, the other name we gave the baby was Amen. Our third daughter is then called "Aviel Amen".

MY FINAL YEAR IN NEGST

He gives strength to the weary and increases the power of the weak. Isaiah 40:29

After a term of maternity leave, I resumed classes in May 1999. It was tough now that I had three children to take care of. The scholarship we were given by the school still only covered tuition so we had to get work scholarships in order to have money for food and other expenses. So not only was the class workload heavy after missing a term but I also had to work. I was dismayed to learn that the library filing work I used to have was no longer available as someone else had that job. My husband used to help with data entry for new library materials but he was also told that he was no longer needed there. We had both lost our "jobs" when we needed them most. We, however, took it positively. The next week we were meeting in our advisory group when I was told that there were some people who had agreed to pay our living expenses for the rest of the time I was going to be in NEGST. I couldn't believe it but then remembered that was only adding to what God had been doing. I was able to enjoy the rest of my time at NEGST knowing that I did not need to struggle for food. Our God was indeed manifesting Himself as our Father just as our daughter's name suggested.

At this point we had not seen any of our family members since 1994 although we had at least had some news. Our old passports were expiring and we were told that we needed to renew them or we could be expelled from the school. At first we did not know what to do. We prayed about it and we were finally convinced. We looked at the whole situation, realizing how things were falling into place. We had enough money to travel and pay for our visas. We thought that this was the time and for sure it was.

Unfortunately, because the second term was beginning a week

later, we had only one week to be in Rwanda, but we were able to get our passports renewed and to see some of our friends and relatives. In 1999, life was slowly coming back. Rebuilding had started especially in the capital city and other towns, but in the rural areas many houses were still in ruins. Roads were still overgrown, especially those which were not tarmacked. Many houses had disappeared and there were vegetable gardens where there used to be a house. The experience was painful but at the same time we were so glad that we were able to go to my father's house and see my father and my mother again and some of my siblings. We just looked at each other for a moment without speaking a word, shedding tears of joy. Time was too short, but the fact that we were able to see each other again was in itself like a dream. Actually after only one hour with them, we had to drive back to Kigali and prepare for our return to Nairobi.

Our term in NEGST was beginning on January 3. I was so tired. I did not have a helper in the house and I was fully loaded with course work. Before long I started feeling uneasy and was unable to eat some foods. I waited for my period but it never came. At the end of January I knew I had conceived again. It was hard. I almost told myself, I am not going to finish, I cannot make it. I simply looked at the work ahead and thought there was no way I could possibly make it. I was depressed. I didn't tell anyone and I started blaming my husband. Aviel was only one year old. She was so affected. I had to take her to the NEGST nursery school where she spent most of the day. She was too young for that but I had no choice. When I later got a house helper, she spent most of her evening with her. The work was just too much for me.

And as if that was not enough, Nairobi experienced water and electricity shortages because of the drought that hit the country that year. There was power rationing and in our area we only had electricity from midnight until 6 a.m. We would do our readings before midnight as we wait for the power to come on so that we could key in our work once it came. It was a tremendous struggle to keep up with everything. My husband was concerned about my health but I also was concerned about my academic work. Sometimes he would hide my books and papers to stop me from going to the computer lab at night. I did not want to delay my graduation. I was not going to be given grace. I had to meet the requirements and the standards set by the college. I thank God who saw me through. I sat for all my exams and passed, finished the two major projects just like my male colleagues and my grades ended up being much better than a number of theirs. On graduation day, July 7, 2000, I was only a month away from my baby's due date. Many, including my lecturers, could not believe I had made it. I remember telling one of them when I was offered a part time job in the Translation Department, that I needed at least few weeks to have my baby, and she was amazed that I had been able to handle all that heavy academic work with a baby on the way. She had never even noticed I was pregnant. I was reminded of David's words that those who sow weeping will reap rejoicing,

Those who sow in tears shall reap in joy.
He who continually goes forth weeping,
Bearing seed for sowing,
Shall doubtless come again with rejoicing,
Bringing his sheaves with him. Psalm 126:5-6

LIFE AFTER NEGST

*For I am the Lord, your God, who takes hold of your
right hand and says to you,*

'Do not fear I will help you'. Isaiah 41:13

After graduation it was time for us to leave. There were so many unknowns in our life! We did not have a specific place where we were going. We were not sure of getting jobs. Our two girls had not yet started primary school and we needed to find a good school for them. I was not sure where my baby was going to be born. NEGST, which had become our home for four years, was now sending us out into the world, a situation we really were not prepared for.

The first step was to look for a house to rent. NEGST had given us a deadline: by August 30 every graduate should have vacated their campus housing. We did not have enough time to shop around. We probably had enough money to rent a house worth KSH 7000 (Kenyan shillings) a month for three months. That did not include food. Our baby was on the way and some shopping had to be done in preparation for the new baby. Aviel was then two years and eight months old. I had carefully kept her baby clothes and wasn't concerned whether the new arrival would be a boy or a girl, I was just glad to have some clothes available. The water shortage continued so we were looking for a place where we at least could have access to water. We found a house in Ngong town, almost 15 km away and in the same compound where two other people from NEGST were renting houses. We felt secure having people around that we knew. That was a key determining factor for us to consider. The rent was KSH 9,000 a month and we were required to pay one month plus a deposit.

On July 31, 2000, we left NEGST and moved to Ngong which was a whole new experience. The people we found in the estate educated us on how to live there. The first scary thing was to learn that the place was not very secure. We were told to always be home before six even if you were driving. Water was insufficient and sanitation was poor. Right behind our house there was a pool of black, smelly water from the poor sewage drainage. We always closed the windows but in vain - the smell was unbearable. The children could not go out and play and the landlord was nowhere to be found. He was a busy businessman who travelled all over the country. I was approaching my due date and there was no hospital in the neighbourhood. We then started wondering what we would do in case of an emergency. I was so scared and I did not want to have my baby in that kind of environment.

During our second week in that house, something terrible happened. Thieves broke into the compound and tried to steal our neighbour's car which was normally parked right by our bedroom windows. Around 3 a.m. we were awakened by the noise as they were trying to get into the car. They tried to start the car but in vain. All the neighbours heard and some of them shouted calling for help. We watched them for about thirty minutes. They finally gave up on taking the car as more people were being alerted, but they stole the car radio, lights and some other parts they managed to remove. No policemen showed up until the next morning. We were all scared by that experience. The children did not want to sleep in their room anymore. We immediately made the decision to move. Within three days we found another house. We hoped to get our money back since we had paid for two months but only stayed for two weeks. Of course the landlord was not willing to do that even though he was an elder in the church. He refused even to give the deposit back but that did not stop us from moving. We knew the God who had been with us before was still keeping His promises.

We found a house in the Kikuyu area not far from Kikuyu hospital. It was a nice compound, they had a water tank and security was much better. I resumed my ante-natal consultation and was expecting the baby about the third week of August. The date came and went but the baby did not come. I started to realize that he or she was not moving as usual so I reported it to the doctor but I was told to go home and wait. At the end of August I went back to the hospital and I expected them to induce me. But they did not want to do it. I was anxious, I was told to count how many kicks I feel every day. They did not even tell me how many were supposed to be normal. On September 12 I woke up very tired and when I went to the bathroom I saw meconium again so I knew the time had come. I went to my bedroom and told my husband that it was time for us to go to the hospital. I packed a few clothes in my bag. Christine came into my bedroom and asked, "Mammy, are you going to bring a baby boy?"

I smiled and said, "Yes" although I did not know what I was getting. I took my Bible and read Psalm 121 and from that moment on I was reciting it in my heart,

> *"I lift my eyes to the hill where does my help come*
> *from? My help comes from the Lord."*

Within a few minutes my husband was back with a taxi to take me to the hospital but I told him I did not need a taxi, I wanted to walk to the hospital to increase contractions and hasten labour.

He said that the taxi was already here and I needed to go in it. I had to obey against my will. When we reached the hospital, I went straight to the clinic and told the nurse that I was coming to deliver my baby. All the nurses looked at me and laughed. They said, 'How do you know it's time?' I explained that I had some discharges in the morning as I went to the bathroom. She could not believe me. I was not in pain. She told me to lie down on the consultation table. She checked and I could read panic on her face. They immediately called the doctor who was attending another patient. She was told there was an emergency so she left the other patient. My clothes were taken off immediately and I was put on IV drips. When I asked what was going on, they said my baby was very distressed and there was no time to lose. I had to be taken to the operating theatre. My husband who was sitting in the waiting room was not even consulted as is usually the norm. As they pushed me into the operating room I was reciting Psalm 121. One of the nurses was praying and I knew I was in good hands. I was taken in at 10 a.m. and at 11:30 I was awake and told I had a baby boy. When I woke up my husband was there with another doctor whom we knew and we had thought he was the one who was going to help us. When he came everything was already done. I was reminded that we do not need to look to men for help. When we look to God alone, He brings people we did not expect and uses them for our good and for His glory. He had done it before, of course, but the unfortunate thing with human beings is that we tend to forget very quickly. His mercies are new every morning and great is His faithfulness.

I was now taken to the general ward which was full of women, most of whom had had surgery. This was quite a new experience for me. Everything had gone well in the operating room but when I was in the ward things were different. The first thing that shocked me was to be told to move by myself from the gurney to my own bed. I told the nurses I wasn't able to do so. One of them abused me but I did not care. In my spirit I was telling myself, "You are a foreigner, what do you expect?" But I heard the same complaint from other women who were from Kenya so I knew it happened to everyone. They finally lifted me from the gurney and put me on another iron bed which was so old that my body was almost sinking into it making my incision very painful. Turning myself was also a problem. I stayed in the same position for almost the whole day. Later I asked for my baby and was told he was in nursery. He was born weak so he had to be kept in a machine. The next day our doctor friend came to see me and I asked him to check on my baby. He came and told me the baby was fine and should be removed from the incubator. He instructed the nurses and they brought him in. He was very thin and hungry. It was very cold and there were a lot of mosquitoes. He caught malaria and a cold but was treated immediately.

We spent three days in the hospital and since our house was not far away they could bring me meals from home. The hospital bill was not too high so we managed to pay.

We did not have a name yet for a boy. When we had Aviel Amen we thought she was the last one. But when the boy came and I had to have surgery, we thought it was a good reason not to plan for another baby. Four was a good number. Every time I was expecting, my husband used to call the unborn baby 'Ben' which was a Hebrew word for son. I knew he wanted a boy so when this baby came he immediately called him Ben as a nickname. When it was time to name him officially, thinking he would be our last child we named him Benjamin. And since he was the only boy and came when we least expected him we also called him Bienvenu meaning welcome. Benjamin was indeed welcomed by his sisters and made a big difference in our family of girls. Interestingly, his father did not show much excitement. I remember whenever I gave birth to the other children my husband always gave me a gift. This time I knew we had financial difficulties but still I thought he would do something. I kept wondering why he didn't give me anything, even a small token. One day I had the courage to ask him and he said, "I did not want you to say that I treated you special because you have given birth to a boy. I love him just like his sisters and wanted you to know that with or without a boy I still appreciate you."

I did not receive many visitors after Ben's birth. Many of our friends did not even know where we lived. But my lecturers Mrs Huttar and Dr. Regina Blass came to see me in the hospital and brought some gifts. I was so happy. Earlier they had given me two big packets of disposable diapers, which I used for at least two months. A few of our other friends came but definitely we could feel the fact that we had left what had become our second family here in Kenya. Once again we felt we were on our own and we had to learn new survival strategies.

Before we left NEGST we had bought a small laptop from a missionary who was returning home. My husband acted as a secretary for a while typing for others in order to earn some money. During this time every kind of job was valuable to us. I took two months to recover and when I was strong enough to walk I had no choice but to go out looking for something to do. The only place I knew was NEGST. But how was I going to get a job there? God was making a way where there seemed to be no way. His mercies were being renewed every day.

TRANSITIONING FROM COLLEGE TO REAL LIFE

Whatever you commanded us we will do, and wherever you send us we will go. Joshua 1:16

When Ben was two months old I decided to visit one of my lecturers. She asked me how we were coping. It was tough of course and I wanted to find out whether it was still possible to find work on campus. She asked whether I would be willing to help in the translation department on a part-time basis. I told her that I would gladly accept the offer. She said she would discuss it with her colleagues who had also been my lecturers. Because they had never had this kind of position at NEGST, they were not sure how to handle it. They needed to define the job description and decide on a salary. Additionally, I did not have a work permit. So they thought I could only work for a certain number of hours a day, and the department was going to pay me based on how many hours I worked at the end of the month. There were no other options open to me at the time, so I took it.

My baby was still too small to begin feeding with formula so I travelled with him every morning to work. My supervisor, Regina Blass gave me a basket which she had bought for her cat but had not yet used. It was Ben's bed in her small office which had temporarily become mine. It was uncomfortable for him but he had to adjust. I wanted him to be at least three months old before being introduced to any other food while I left him at home. Aviel was also very small, only 1 year and 10 months old, and she needed a lot of attention. When Ben turned three months old, I started leaving him and took Aviel with me. Fortunately there was a nursery school at NEGST and she could be there during the day giving me time to concentrate on my work in the office.

In the evening, on our way home I had to pass by Sandrine

and Christine's school to fetch them. The school was far from home and they were too young to come home on their own. I also didn't trust the house girls enough to let them go to pick them up. My husband had begun studying for his second masters' degree at the Nairobi International School of Theology, almost 20 km away from NEGST and about 5 km away from the city centre. He always came home late so he couldn't fetch the girls either. I had to make sure all the children were well taken care of. It was a major challenge having nearly all the household responsibilities for a family of six on my shoulders. How did I manage it? Only God knows.

All of 2001 was a year of many struggles. But the administration of Nairobi International School of Theology helped us time and again once my husband became one of their students. Sometimes we had no food in the house because whatever I got from NEGST was used to pay the rent. But whenever my husband went to them they always helped and we as a family felt like we were part of them. Seeing how we were struggling, they offered to give us a house, free of charge in Santack Estate. At the end of May 2001 we moved from Kikuyu town, almost 20 miles from Nairobi to our new house. This made our lives much easier. There was a nursery school within the estate and Aviel transferred there. Christine and Sandrine moved to a nearby school and the school bus picked them up right from home. It was much easier for my husband to go to NIST together with his colleagues who had become our new neighbours. Going to NEGST was not a problem for me anymore and Ben could be left at home with a house girl or the neighbours. What a relief! Our financial problems hadn't gone away, but our lives were back on track. Everyone seemed to enjoy what she or he was doing.

In the meantime I met Dr. Payne, a lecturer from Oregon University who was working on a Maasai dictionary. She wanted me to help in entering some Maa texts in the database and paid me for this work. Her pay doubled what I was earning in the translation department. With the improved income things were better and soon a number of people asked me to translate or proofread their materials. All of a sudden I had too much on my plate but at the end of the day, I put food on the table. My life went on like that until June 2002 when I learned that the Translation department at Pan Africa Christian University (or PAC) was looking for an African lecturer since up until then the department had only missionaries on the teaching staff. It is located in the eastern part of Nairobi, about 10 km from the city centre. I was approached by SIL and persuaded to apply. With much hesitation from PAC university administration I was taken in as a part-time lecturer teaching only one course in September 2002.

It was hard to believe that someone like me who less than five years earlier was unable to formulate a complete English sentence was now going to lecture in English. My colleagues weren't so sure either knowing that I had done most of my studies in a language other than English. One of them was to sit in my class at least for the first year. I had no problem with that. I began with a lot of fear and I did not trust myself. I had taught before but not at the university level and not in English. You should have seen me the first morning, as I wondered what clothes and shoes to put on. Since there weren't many options available it ultimately made my choice easier.

I did not know which *matatu* (minibus) to board and where to find it. I was completely ignorant; downtown Nairobi was completely unfamiliar to me since I always went there with other people. On the first day my husband had to accompany me and help me find my way. I was afraid I would be late for my first class but I made it just in time, around 9:30 a.m. Two gates lead into the college's compound. The first gate led to Evangel Publishing House and the second led to PAC but I did not know which to use. When I went to Evangel's gate the watchman could not let me in. I begged him but in vain. I rushed to the other gate and since the watchman did not know me it took some minutes to identify myself. In the process I ended up being a few minutes late but Bill Gardner who was supposed to take me into the classroom was standing outside waiting for me. I was sweating, my heart was beating in an unusual way, but I tried to hide my feelings. In class, Bill introduced me as the new lecturer and after he distributed the syllabi for me, he left. Once everyone else had introduced themselves I gave my first lesson. My prior teaching skills and experience helped a lot and the students were kind enough. Probably the fact of seeing a new face, the first African lecturer teaching in the department, helped to capture their attention. In the end I enjoyed it and told myself, "I can do this!"

It was Tuesday, so I had to go to Chapel. Elizabeth Olsen who was the head of our department urged me to be there for the introduction. Pastor Anataka who was then the chaplain introduced everyone else, mostly students, but not me. It seemed strange. I thought he forgot, but it never happened afterwards. For more than a year only the students who I taught knew me. I remember one day sitting in the cafeteria when a student asked me, "Which year are you?" I smiled and told him I was a teacher. He apologized but I told him it was fine. In the staff tea room not many people knew me either. Since I had not been formally introduced, I found myself answering the same questions from different people at different times. What do you do here? Which part of Kenya do you come from? Are you an SIL lecturer? How did you get the job? Do you teach PAC courses or SIL courses? Who pays you?

In the tea room, my African colleagues would speak their languages that I did not speak. I tended to feel lonely unless a *Mzungu* (name given to a white person in Africa) was around so that English would be spoken.

In August 2003, after I had taught for a year, PAC decided to seek a work permit for me. One of the most disturbing questions that a colleague asked was, "I understand the college is looking for a work permit for you. How are they going to explain that there is no Kenyan who can do the job?" I was disturbed but after a short moment God gave me an answer. I told the person, "It is possible that there are many Kenyans who can do the job I am doing, but if we believe we are all God's children and He does not show favouritism, then if He thinks I am the person to do the job now, no one else will have it and He will release the work permit." I went on to say, "God is never bound to man's policies. He follows His own policy." The conversation ended there and

I was left wondering where I got the confidence to respond like that. The answer was very simple. As I remembered the great things God had done before, I knew that He was still in control.

In February 2004, to my surprise and the surprise of many others, God released the work permit. And just like the psalmist says, *"Our mouth was filled with laughter and our tongue with singing" Psalm 126: 2*

The process of having the permit endorsed in my passport took another three months and finally on May 1, 2004, I began my job as a full time lecturer with all the privileges pertaining to the position.

LIFE IN PAN AFRICA CHRISTIAN UNIVERSITY (PAC)

"You will keep in perfect peace him whose mind is steadfast, because he trusts in you." Isaiah 26:3

Before I began full time teaching, we were living in a very small two-bedroom house given to us by NIST. Whenever we had a guest, our daughter Christine, would ask if the visitor was going to spend the night. She was stressed. She did not like having to move from the bedroom to the sitting room, nor did the children like to have a stranger sleeping with them in the same room. We knew it was hard but it was unavoidable. When I was told we could move to the PAC campus I did not hesitate.

Based on the size of our family, we were given a four bedroom house which was the largest one on campus. When I was taken to tour the house I was in disbelief. My only question was how to get furniture to put in there. We only had one bed and some mattresses and no money to buy beds, sofas or tables. Elizabeth put a note in the SIL newsletter asking who might have furniture to lend or sell or give away. We received an immediate reply from the SIL Congo branch. They had some old sofas, beds, tables, desks and shelves in their store and did not know what to do with them. They were initially bought for some of their students from Congo who came without English and had to spend some months in Nairobi taking English classes with their families before being accepted by NEGST. The branch was willing to let us have them and we saw this as another provision from God. In fact when God is leading you somewhere, He makes all things fall into place in ways that you would have never imagined.

On April 30, 2004, we moved and life became different. Water was plentiful and clean so that we didn't have to boil our drinking water anymore. We learned how to take hot showers instead of baths. There was space enough for everyone. I had to struggle to keep Ben and Aviel who were 4 and 5 years old, respectively, from playing football in the house. For them the sitting room seemed large enough for that. While Sandrine and Christine enjoyed sleeping in their own beds, Ben and Aviel didn't like to feel lonely in bed. I had to train them to sleep by themselves. They often asked me whether we would ever go back home (i.e., to the previous house). They did not yet feel that this was our new home. I, on the other hand, woke up every day humbled by God's faithfulness. He provides refuge, help, and comfort for those who trust in Him. And through trust, humility, and obedience we enjoy the comfort of God's refuge even in a foreign land.

When I was teaching on part-time basis I did not have enough time to interact with many people And I had not felt like I was a true part of the community. I had many things to learn now about this new community where we lived and I worked. I was told many stories such as, "Here in PAC we do not go knocking on people's doors. Do not expect people to come to your house. Africans do not mix with *Wazungus.* At first I tended to believe all that I had been told while also observing to see whether it was true or not. In May 2004, my husband graduated from NIST. I invited everyone and although no one from PAC attended, at least I was given the school van to take my family to the function and back, free of charge. I was allowed to use the cafeteria to prepare some of my food and felt great encouragement from the cafeteria staff. In the evening I had all my colleagues from the translation department come for fellowship.

While we were celebrating the graduation, something tragic had happened back in Rwanda but we did not find out until three days later. My father passed away but the message took all that time to reach us. It was a bad time for me and I needed people to be with me and my family. I also had to find a way to go home. Most of my colleagues and my immediate neighbours were African but very few came to express their condolences. Even the person who had told me most of the stories about how unchristian the PAC community was did not come. Being an African myself, I did not blame the white people so much but I could not understand the aloofness of my fellow Africans. I went home for the funeral and when I came back I continued to be surprised that no one told me they were sorry to hear about my father's death. That was the toughest time I had in PAC. Bitterness was starting to take hold. I could not appreciate almost anything. I kept comparing PAC with some of the other places where I had lived before. I thought everyone was my enemy and even felt like packing up and leaving.

What began feeling like a blessing had in a short time, turned into a nightmare.

This continued until August 2004, when the principal took the whole staff on a retreat. This became a turning point in my life at PAC. We spent the whole day in a series of activities and the last event on the agenda was Holy Communion. It was organized in a very unique and powerful way. For the first time since I joined PAC I experienced the power of the Holy Spirit in that setting.

The principal distributed the bread and asked us to meet in small groups of two or three. We were supposed to share our experiences and pray for one another. I did not join any group. One woman noticed I was alone so she joined me in a corner of the room. We started sharing and praying. In that moment I felt the pain of unforgiveness. I was convinced that something was wrong with me. I started crying. I made a simple prayer to God and asked my friend to pray for me, too. My prayer was:

God, help me to do what is right even if I feel I do not want to

Give me love especially for those I feel I cannot love

Help me to accept people the way they are and appreciate them.

While I prayed I mentioned a few names in my heart. From that time on things were different. I knew I had to show love to people so I visited some of my colleagues whenever they were grieving or sick. As a result I experienced peace, joy and excitement. Before long I was invited to attend a weekly Bible group for women. Most of the participants were missionaries and I was the only African although another joined later. I was blessed through the Bible study. I felt loved and cared for. What joy when we make it a priority to follow and to live according to God's Word. And the Word of God is true, we reap what we sow (Galatians 6:7) and all of us will have to give an account of our own deeds before the throne. We must be willing to give other people what we would like to get from them. Love is not conditional and being a Christian doesn't make us a judge.

TWO MORE WERE BORN

Are you ever burdened with a load of care?
Does the cross seem heavy you are called to bear?
Count your many blessings, ev'ry doubt will fly
And you will be singing as the days go by.[9]

In these days when many think that children are a burden they do not want to bear, I count them as the most precious gifts that God has given me. The pain and the expense it takes to bear them and to bring them up are unimportant because I know that the Author of life will take care. There is a reason why God chose me to be an instrument for expanding His creation. I see it as a privilege. After experiencing surgery when giving birth to Ben, I thought I would never travel that road again. But that was not God's plan. In August 2004, I had a routine visit to the gynaecologist who told me that I had a serious problem which needed to be taken care of. Eventually some minor surgery was performed and cost quite a lot of money. A month after the operation I realized I was expecting. My gynaecologist who was a Christian looked at me after giving me the results of my test and asked me what I was feeling right then. I responded that I was confused. She looked into my eyes and said, "Do you know what? You are not the one who gives life. The life in you does not belong to you but to God. So relax, the Giver of life is in control."

Simple as they were, these words ministered to me in a very special way. My only worry was in thinking about how I was going to break the news to my colleagues. Lori and Bill Gardner were to leave in July 2005 and my baby was due at almost the same time which meant I would not be able to teach the following term. We were also expecting David and Estelle Abernathy to join us in August 2005 and Helen Wilson had also been wanting to come as it was not possible for her to go to Cote d' Ivoire where she had worked before.

The evening when I met with Elizabeth Olsen at her house is memorable. We were having a nice chat over a cup of tea and in my mind I was trying to think of the words to use to break the news. When I did, I was very surprised to see that she was excited. She told me that many people would like to have children but are not able to. She said I should not blame myself but just accept this as God's blessing. What a relief! Now we were able to plan. Her greatest problem had been how she was going to be able to give everyone enough teaching hours. This, then, was God's answer for her and also for me.

On Saturday, August 6, 2005, I had a house full of visitors and was up and down all day. At night I felt very tired. Our neighbour Pastor Mugambi, then academic dean of PAC, came to our house and told us that whenever we needed to go to the hospital we could call him at any time. We were surprised. Later that same night I could not sleep and was in a lot of pain but did not want to disturb anyone, not even my husband. At around 5 a.m. I couldn't take it anymore so I woke my husband and asked him to call Pastor Mugambi. He was ready in a few seconds and they took me to Mater Hospital where I had been attending the clinic. I was admitted and put on a machine to monitor the baby's heart beat. It was so irregular and the doctor said that was a sign that the baby was tired. They did not want to take any chances so they immediately took me to the operating theatre. On Sunday, August 7, Vickie was born. God was with me, because in the process of recovering from the anaesthesia, the nurses removed the oxygen mask before I was able to breathe fully on my own. I remember struggling and hearing them shouting saying, "Now what is it?" and another said, "She cannot breathe."

They put the mask back on and when I was finally awake I asked about my baby. They constantly told me the baby was fine and that I should keep quiet. But I could not stop shouting praises to my God for protecting me. I only spent two nights in the hospital because I was worried about the bill. I did not have medical coverage and I knew what it meant to have an operation in Nairobi. Though I was not strong I had to leave the hospital. Even though I spent as little time as possible in the hospital, the bill was a shock. It came to around $1500 and yet a lady whose bed was next to mine, had had surgery and had been in the hospital for nine days, and her bill was much lower than mine. I was upset but took it easy. The University had to pay for me and in turn they would recover their money through my salary. All that did not matter because I was alive and my baby was well. Until the termination of my contract I continued struggling to pay off that debt, but God saw me through.

I remembered the words that my sister-in-law had shared when she came for my husband's graduation. In her speech she had said, "In everything always remember that Jesus knows those that are His and He never forsakes them." I kept those words in my heart and I had thought that if I were to have another baby I would call her/him Yesazabe or in short Azabe. So when Vickie (name given by my husband) was born I declared this and those words were alive and I decided to call her Azabe, as a name which literally means "He (Jesus) knows His (people)." And for sure He knows us. He has never failed to show that He knows us and that He keeps us in His mind; we are always visible to Him. What a privilege!

Helen Wilson ended up only staying at PAC for a term because she had to leave to take care of her father but while she was there she covered all my courses while I was on maternity leave. I was amazed once again at how God makes His own arrangements and His plans work perfectly.

Our last baby, Regina Mwizere, was born April 12, 2007. At this time it was almost certain that my job at PAC was ending. There were a lot of uncertainties, but thank God for the people in the Translation Department. David Abernathy's family and Elizabeth Olsen will be forever remembered in our family. Their moral, emotional, and financial support was incredible. I thank Liz for standing with me even when I was not aware, together with her church in the UK who provided a salary for the three months I worked in PAC University prior to the official dismissal. May the Lord enrich you. Let the Lord Who sees what is done in secret, reward you.

How did we come up with Regina's name? One of the people who impacted my life and who played a big role in my healing process was Professor Regina Blass. She was my lecturer, tutor, friend and a sister. The only way we could honour her was to name one of our children after her. Her second name, Mwizere, which means "believe" or have "faith" was to remind us that even though the road was not clear, we knew this was the time to once again exercise our faith for a new bright future. As John MacArthur says,

The Lord wants the experience, though perhaps difficult as we pass through it, to be a positive one in the end—one that strengthens and refines our faith. [10]

My contract was coming to an end, my husband was jobless, we had six children to feed and four to send to school. We had no house and were still paying off a heavy medical bill …the list goes on and on. In the eyes of men things were tough. But we kept reminding ourselves where we had come from and we knew the Lord was involved in the whole process. It was time to demonstrate the validity of what we professed, not merely to imitate what others do or say.

In September 2007, when the new academic year began, it was very clear that my contract would not be renewed and a dismissal letter was given to me by the Vice Chancellor. This was not good news! As my mind wrestled trying to come to terms with the situation, many questions flooded my mind and at the same time God ministered to me and my family. We did not allow the spirit of discouragement, bitterness and confusion to take root. Instead we continued to encourage one another and we also had friends around us who helped make our lives easier and enjoyable. Thank God for the Ladies' Bible study. Whenever I was weak they made me strong, if discouraged, they gave a word of encouragement, if hungry, they fed my family. In short they surrounded us with love, joy and peace. All my colleagues were concerned and everyone was willing to help. To us that was a confirmation that God was in control of the whole situation, and for sure He was.

When I was asked to speak in the University Chapel, I remember heading to my office wondering what message to leave with those who would be there. I opened my Bible and my eyes went to Genesis 21:8-20 where Hagar and Ishmael were being sent away from Abraham's house. As I read the story, I was moved by the way God intervened in Hagar and Ishmael's situation. In the midst of their misery He came to give them hope. He gave them a promise that He would care for them and expand them. And for Him to do that He had to take them out of their comfort zone. Those promises became mine and I knew that I was not only expecting a well in the wilderness but a stream, a very big stream indeed. And for sure from that time on we begun to see the Lord's blessing flowing, day by day and we have no doubt that for the rest of our lives we live to enjoy the blessings of the Lord and at the same time blessing His people. We know the journey is still long, but the good thing is we are not travelling alone. God is with us.

NEW OPPORTUNITIES

When upon life's billows you are tempest tossed,
When you are discouraged, thinking all is lost,
Count your blessings, name them one by one,
And it will surprise you what the Lord has done. [11]

Indeed the Lord kept surprising me after I stopped teaching full time. Right away I was called to teach a course at Jomo Kenyatta University of Agriculture and Technology from May to August 2008. At the same time I was listed as adjunct faculty at PAC University and given the opportunity to teach courses I had never taught before. A number of these were Bible courses. It was a time for me to grow and I could already see God expanding me by making me cross into unfamiliar but not unknown territory. Until 2009, as I was concluding this book I was still teaching at PAC University. I would like to thank Professor Lilian Wahome for giving me that opportunity. She was like a caring mother. For sure in tough times some will try to pull you down into the pit, but many will be used to pull you up.

One morning in November 2008, as I was going to work a friend called and told me about an organization that was holding a workshop and looking for facilitators. She sent me the contact person's information and I called. I was urged to go to their office and immediately I was given an assignment to train young leaders from five different African countries in peace, justice, conflict management and conflict resolution, and leadership. The organization is called FECCLAHA. It was such a good new exposure for me, a very enriching experience. Through that workshop, I began to reflect on the role of our African cultures in generating conflicts and I was left with a burden to do further research in this area. I know there might be a lot of reports on the subject produced by big world organizations, but I am convinced that if Africa is to live in peace and harmony, the church has a big role to play. Yet many times we as the church may not have what it takes to accomplish our role. One reason is lack of accurate information and lack of awareness. Many times we believe what our cultures have taught us even when they are not in agreement with what the Scriptures say. That had become very clear to me and I decided I would carry out some research to help the church in Africa and in the rest of world.

Another surprise came in December 2008 when I received an invitation to attend an international conference in Switzerland. I thought it was crazy to even think about going but God used my mentor Regina Blass and the church in Germany to take care of all the expenses in order to allow me attend. Wycliffe Germany was willing to provide all the necessary papers to help with the visa process. I had no words to express my gratitude. And this only confirmed all the promises that God gave us and the assurance that He was and is still with us in the wilderness.

In February I attended the conference and spent a week in Germany. I made many friends, interacted with a number of women, and visited churches. And in all that I saw that the favour of the Lord was upon me.

Now as I conclude this book, which I trust is only the beginning of what God has for us, I would like to encourage every reader who comes across this book with a very simple message: NEVER, EVER GIVE UP - GOD IS FAITHFUL!

FAITH LESSONS
LEARNED

Mine is a story of hope. After taking you with me along the road of life that the Lord has caused me to travel so far, it is appropriate to end this book by highlighting some of the lessons learned. It is my prayer that as you read it you will also realize that the trials we go through are simply used as refiners of our faith. As John MacArthur has said,

"Experience is the hardest teacher. It gives the test first, then the lesson. Therefore we should approach them with a positive attitude."[12]

The following are some of my lessons learned and hopefully at the end of the day they will speak to you. Through suffering everything is made new: new foundations, new expectations and longings, new fulfilments, new ways of thinking.

1. Through suffering I received assurance that the God of my salvation and confidence cares about me. Certainly when I was going through everything that I described in this story, I had moments when I thought that I would never have an opportunity to be happy and enjoy life. When all that you have worked for is gone, you have no family around you, your education becomes useless, you have no place to sleep, you cannot even feed yourself or your family, and even your identity is compromised, it is very hard for anyone to think that it is possible to be happy and have joy. But then I saw my God giving me back, in His own way, everything that I had lost. As one author has said,

"Your deepest joy comes when you have nothing around you to bring outward pleasure and Jesus becomes your total joy"[13]

I have learned that there is no mathematical formula for this to happen. It takes patience, perseverance and faith. I have learned to choose to have the right attitude in all circumstances. When you know that God is not caught by surprise no matter what situation you find yourself in, then you are able to move forward with hope. As John MacArthur states,

> *"Our joy will not always be automatic and we can not deny that real pain and sorrow accompanies suffering, but in the long run it's a matter of which way we look."*[14]

I have chosen not to look at the negative side of my circumstances and not to allow them to steal the joy that is mine. After all it is the only thing we have that is eternal. When our time comes we won't take our material wealth, nor our academic degrees, nor our beautiful houses or cars, nor our friends and relatives unless they are saved, we will not need our race or tribesmen. Why should we allow all those temporal things to steal what is eternal, our heavenly inheritance? It is not easy, of course, and we are reminded by Carol Kent that since we are not alone in our struggle, we have to direct our longings in the right direction.

2. Suffering leads us into spiritual growth. As the book of James says:

> *"Consider it all joy, my brethren when you encounter various trials, knowing that the testing of your faith produces endurance. And let endurance have its perfect result, that you may be perfect and complete, lacking in nothing."* James 1:2-4

I have seen the truth of James' words in my life. The fact that I am even able to write this book is a testimony to that. I mentioned earlier how I learnt English and later went to school for my postgraduate studies. It took a lot of patience, endurance and courage to be able to do that. And above all it confirms that God is always with us through our suffering so that He may glorify Himself. Living a life that is pleasing to God is a way of finding true comfort in Him no matter what.

There is always a path He would like us to follow. Sometimes it is rough. You may not see much farther than the point you are at right now. But God expects you to move at His pace, watching and following Him for direction. The butterfly's story I used at the beginning is revealing. We need to understand that sometimes the opening God wants us to squeeze through is very tiny and very uncomfortable. That tiny opening requires much patience and endurance. But unless God Himself gives us another option we should not seek our own option.

We have the example of Abraham, a man of great faith, chosen and blessed by God, a man of righteousness. But although he had received many promises from God, one day he was convinced by his beloved wife Sarah to do something which was against God's will and which brought trouble not only to him and his family but also to his extended descendents. He was promised a son in his old age, but not seeing tangible progress, he thought he and his wife Sarah could chose to do it another way. At Sarah's urging, Abraham slept with Hagar and Ishmael was born. He and Sarah did not wait long enough, God had mercy on him but he had to face the consequences which we are still dealing with even today.

Of course one of the promises was about the Land. Abraham's descendents were only able to see that land after several centuries. But before they got there, they had to go through a lot of struggles.

I give thanks to the Lord who has helped us to persevere as we squeeze through the opening which He meant for us. Once we get through, there is no doubt we will be better people, people of God's design and making. And that is my prayer for the children that He has blessed us with. We pray that they may become living testimonies of what God alone can do.

3. Suffering takes you from your self-made comfort zone to a God-made comfort zone. Someone has said that a comfort zone is a dead zone. Indeed renewed life in Christ, a proper understanding of what it means to be in relationship with God the Father, realizing the potential I had to grow higher than where I was up until 1994 only took place after I had been taken out of my comfort zone. Many people do not know what it looks like to live outside your own country, away from your home and all that is familiar. Going from the known to the unknown comes with a lot of fear. But remember that from the Old to the New Testament, no one who was used in God's mission did so without being moved out of their comfort zone. God took Abraham, Joseph, Moses, David, Joshua, Jesus Himself, and His disciples out of their comfort zones. Why do we think that it should be done differently for us? It seems you are able to discover who you really are when the only person left that you can identify with is Christ Himself. He alone is complete, He alone has everything you need, He alone is the true friend in all seasons, and He makes all His friends become yours. Maybe you are in the midst of your trials and persecutions and you feel lonely and discouraged, are you able to identify yourself with Christ?

4. Suffering creates new values in your life including humility. Have you ever felt good about yourself, what you have achieved, the kind of family you have, the position you hold in the society. These are some of the things that had taken the place of God in my life. They had become the source of my pride. Having been able to earn a degree in a country where very few women did so at that time, having married a Christian husband, having a good job, I could only see a brilliant future. But in one day all this (except my husband, of course) was gone and life was never the same again.

While it is true that disasters, wars, disease affect people of all classes, it only sticks in our minds when we are personally affected. Believers are not spared. In every case loss brings humiliation in people's lives. Therefore I have learned not to hold tightly to anything on this earth. I have decided not to take pride in anything else apart from Christ. And the scriptures say, *"Humble yourself before the Lord and He will lift you up"* James 4:10.

Everything that I have is only temporary. I have chosen to accept whatever God brings my way with a joyful attitude and to respond submissively. Only then have I been able to receive

God's help and see His providence working in my situation.

This anonymous author's words describe my own situation and maybe yours too:

I asked for Strength...
And God gave me Difficulties to make me strong.

I asked for Wisdom...
And God gave me Problems to solve.

I asked for prosperity....
And God gave me a Brain and Brawn to work.

I asked for Courage...
And God gave me Obstacles to overcome.

I asked for Love...
And God gave me troubled people to help.

I asked for Favors...
And God gave me Opportunities.

"I received nothing I wanted...
But I received everything I needed."

5. **Suffering helps you fit in your own shoes.** Many disappointments we encounter in life come from the fact that we define who we are based on other people's standards. We want to be like them and have what they have. Through my journey I have learned to be who I am, not someone else.

God created each one of us in a very unique way. We are special. But in order to be what God meant us to be we have to learn to walk into our own shoes which cannot fit anyone else. Before 1994 I was walking in shoes I had made for myself. I liked them. I thought they fitted me very well. I was comfortable. I did not wish to lose them. But after 1994, God gave me new shoes. Like any pair of new shoes they were not always comfortable. They had not yet moulded to my feet and my feet needed to be flexible enough to conform to the new shoes. The learning was slow, sometimes painful, but finally I adjusted. I am now walking tall in my shoes. I like them because they are from God. Many people come and ask me my secret, they wonder how I manage to do the things I do; those who know ask how I manage to keep the calm. The answer is simple, I learned to walk in my own shoes.

My Shoes

Thank God for my shoes-they fit.

I woke up one day and I realized that there were many things about my life I was not satisfied with or better still, there were challenges that were threatening my soul.

And I said to myself, "Why should anyone envy me and want to be in my shoes." They don't know how far I've come, they don't know what lies ahead of me, and neither do they know how dissatisfied I get with myself from time to time.

People don't know the troubles that you've had or the price you had to pay to get to where you are. All they want to know is that they wish they were like you.

Why should you wish you were in anybody's shoes when you hardly know how they fit?

When you've worn your shoes for a while, they take the shape of your feet and align to the way you walk. If you were to wear my shoes, you will not be comfortable in them.

So I stopped wishing that I am in someone else shoes because it might not fit!

I have learned to be best in what I do, and I know no-one can replace me anywhere and in any sphere.

I am the original, my God is not in the cloning business. He makes originals!

Make the best of what you do; besides you have this beautiful life to live ONLY ONCE.

Live it to the fullest.

(Anonymous)

6. **If you want God to intervene in your situation of suffering no matter how painful it might be, stop blaming other people, take responsibility.** Start by asking God to show you the way out of that situation. If we keep our eyes fixed on people, not only will we be disappointed but we also close off the door of blessings. Only when someone has experienced a similar situation can they truly understand what you are going through. And so the responses of others might be slow or inappropriate or ineffective. But when you leave it to God, He

has full understanding of what is going on, He understands your pain because He has suffered. He understands what it means to be without a home or without food. He understands the pain of losing a close friend or relative and the pain of being rejected. He suffered all that. And what did He do? He went to the Father in prayer. When He was rejected He showed love. Follow His example. He is our hope and our help - our tribe, our family, our government, our job, our education, our social status. None of these will provide us with the help we need. Our God embraces everyone without boundaries.

7. **Suffering tests the strength and quality of your foundation**. The Bible talks about the strength of building on solid rock:

> *"The rain came down, the streams rose, and the*
> *winds blew and beat against that house; yet it did*
> *not fall because it had its foundation on the rock."*
> Matthew 7:27

I realized that my foundation was built partly on rock and partly on sand. When it was shaken I had to deal with the cheap materials that I had initially used and replace them with those of greater value. I needed a paradigm shift in most areas of my life. Our marriage was not spared either. The rain, the storms and the winds beat it also. But we thank God that it resisted all those. The more it was hit the more we worked on it to make it stronger. Today we may not be wealthy, we live a normal, simple life, but God has given joy that can only be found in Him. We are no longer afraid of the storms, no matter how strong they might be because we are standing on a solid rock. I do not intend to say that we no longer have hardships. But we know there is no storm that Christ is not aware of. We had to learn to get closer to Him and to trust Him even in the simple things. My heart is in agreement with the writer of the song "Trust and Obey" and I pray that these words may become mine till my days are over.

Trust and obey
For there is no other way
To be happy in Jesus
And to trust and obey.

When we walk with the Lord
In the light of His Word
What a glory He sheds on our way!
When we do His good will,
He abides with us still
And with all who will trust and obey.

Not a shadow can rise,
Not a cloud in the skies,
But His smile quickly drives it away!
Not a doubt nor a fear,
Not a sigh nor a tear,
Can abide while we trust and obey.

Not a burden we bear,

Not a sorrow we share,

But our toil He doth richly repay!

Not a grief nor a loss,

Not a frown nor a cross

But is blest if we trust and obey

But we never can prove,

The delights of His love

Until all on the altar we lay;

For the favour He shows,

And the joy He bestows

Are for those who will trust and obey.

Then in fellowship sweet

We will sit at His feet,

Or we will walk by His side in the way;

What He says we will do,

Where He sends we will go,

Never fear, only trust and obey. [15]

As I finish my book I would like to end with a special encouragement to every woman who would read it. The following thoughts from an unknown author say it all:

The Woman

When God created woman he was working late on the 6th day

An angel came by and said: "Why spend so much time on that one?"

And the Lord answered:

"Have you seen all the specifications I have to meet to shape her?"

"She must be washable, but not made of plastic, have more than 200 moving parts which all must be replaceable and she must function on all kinds of food, she must be able to embrace several kids at the same time, give a hug that can heal anything from a bruised knee to a broken heart and she must do all this with only two hands".

The angel was impressed.

"Just two hands....impossible! "

And this is the standard model?!

"Too much work for one day....wait until tomorrow and then complete her".

"I will not", said the Lord. "I am so close to completing this creation, which will be the favourite of my heart".

"She cures herself when sick and she can work 18 hours a day".

The angel came nearer and touched the woman.

"But you have made her so soft, Lord"

"She is soft", said the Lord, "But I have also made her strong. You can't imagine what she can endure and overcome."

"Can she think?" the angel asked.

The Lord answered:

"Not only can she think, she can reason and negotiate."

The angel touched the woman's cheek....

"Lord, it seems this creation is leaking! You have put too many burdens on her."

"She is not leaking....it's a tear," the Lord corrected the angel

"What's it for?" asked the angel.

And the Lord said:

"Tears are her way of expressing grief, her doubts, her love, her loneliness, her suffering and her pride."

This made a big impression on the angel; "Lord, you are a genius.

You thought of everything. The woman is indeed marvellous!"

Indeed she is!

Woman has strengths that amazes man. She can handle trouble and carry heavy burdens.

She holds happiness, love and opinions.

She smiles when feeling like screaming.

She sings when she feels like crying, cries when she is happy and laughs when she is afraid.

She fights for what she believes in.

Stand up against injustice.

She doesn't take "no" for an answer, when she can see a better solution. She gives herself so her family can thrive. She takes her friend to the doctor if she is afraid.

Her love is unconditional.

She cries when her kids are victorious. She is happy when her friends do well.

She is glad when she hears of a birth or a wedding.

Her heart is broken when a next of kin or friend dies.

But she finds the strength to get on with life.

She knows that a kiss and a hug can heal a broken heart.

There is only one thing wrong with her

"She forgets what she is worth…!"

Epilogue

The author of the book, together with her husband, has been living in Kenya since 1995. God has blessed them with five daughters, Sandrine, Christine, Aviel, Vicky and Regina and a son named Benjamin.

She tells her story of how God led them as a family, providing for and protecting them in difficult times. It is a story of God's faithfulness in the midst of hopelessness. The purpose of the book is to encourage those who may be wondering and asking many questions about their own situations.

In Africa today complex and pervasive political conflicts have created huge social and economic problems. Many have been left without homes. The number of orphans and widows is growing. Women are agonizing and are left without protection and support, and yet they are supposed to be the pillars, not only of their families but also of their communities. Those who have been forced to leave their home country are struggling with identity and have lost their dignity. Families are no longer in harmony because the natural order does not seem to apply anymore; adjustments are not easy in many cases. Fathers are no longer able to protect and provide for their families. Children are not given the care that is due to them. In the midst of all this a sensation of hopelessness sets in. In this book the author describes how, in spite of the struggles and the difficulties, God has changed her once miserable situation into opportunities for strength and growth and ministry.

Problems will arise, life will not be always easy but we should not stay in the problem. Take steps of faith, remain faithful to your God and He will see you through.

In one of his aired programmes, Pastor John Hagee of Cornerstone Church in San Antonio, Texas, USA, suggested seven things that can help shorten your stay in the problem:

1. Acknowledge the problem

2. Take responsibility. You are "Response' able for you to take control of your life

3. Be willing to work

4. When you are wrong, admit it

5. Accept God's forgiveness

6. Control your tongue

7. Get off your pity pot

END NOTES

1. Bridgers, cited by David Roper (2009), *'Sing!'* In Our Daily Bread (Oct 1st), Michigan: RBC Ministries.

2. Cooper, Darien B. (1974), *You Can Be the Wife of A Happy Husband: Discovering the Key to Marital Success.* Weaton: Victor Books, p.81

3. Muindi, Florence, (2998), *The Pursuit of His Calling: Following in Purpose.* Wakeforest: IPI Integrity Publishers.

4. Shisholm, Thomas O. (1969). *'Great is your Faithfulness'* In Hymns of Glorious Praise, Springfield, Missouri: Gospel Publishing House.

5. Haan, D. De cited by Vernon Grounds (2008), *'Where was God'* In Our Daily Bread (Aug.31st), Michigan: RBC Ministries

6. Roper, David, (2008), *'Anywhere with Jesus'* In Our Daily Bread (Sept. 9th), Michigan : RBC Ministries

7. Eastman, Dick and Jack Hayford, (1988), *Living and Praying in Jesus Name.* Wheaton: Tyndale House Publishers, p.82

8. Grounds, Vernon (2008), *'Inner Peace'* In Our Daily Bread (Aug. 22nd), Michigan: RBC Ministries.

9. Oatman, Johnson (1969), *'Count Your Blessings'* In Hymns of Glorious Praise, Springfield, Missouri: Gospel Publishing House

10. MacArthur, John (1995), *The Power of Suffering: Strengthening your Faith in the Refiner's Fire.* USA: Victor's Books, p.13.

11. Oatman, Johnson (1969), *'Count Your Blessings'* In Hymns of Glorious Praise, Springfield, Missouri: Gospel Publishing House.

12. MacArthur, John (1995), *The Power of Suffering: Strengthening your Faith in the Refiner's Fire.* USA: Victor Books, p. 13

13. Kent, Carol (1990). *Secrets Longings of the Heart. Overcoming Disappointment and unfulfilled Expectations.* Colorado Springs: NavPressp.32.

14. MacArthur, John (1995), *The Power of Suffering: Strengthening your Faith in the Refiner's Fire.* USA: Victor's Books, p.140

15. Sammis, John H. (1969) *'Trust and Obey'* In Hymns of Glorious Praise, Springfield, Missouri: Gospel Publishing House.

The information contained in this book is exclusively taken from personal experience and no one is permitted to reproduce or distribute any part of it without prior consultation with the author. To contact the author, write to cnyiramahoro@yahoo.com